INTERNET & NETWORK SECURITY

The Practical Guide to Internet and Network Security

From Business Objectives to Operational Defense

FIRST EDITION

A comprehensive treatment of security strategy, encryption, identity, firewall architecture and policy, encrypted-traffic inspection, zero trust and SASE, DNS and email defense, network and wireless attacks, endpoint and application security, security operations and orchestration, incident response and malware analysis, and the emerging challenges of artificial intelligence and quantum computing.

Payam Hojjat, M.S., CISSP

The Practical Guide to Internet and Network Security

From Business Objectives to Operational Defense — First Edition

Typeset in Georgia and Arial. Figures and tables prepared for this edition.

Contents

Preface

Most security books fall into one of two traps. They either drown you in checklists with no explanation of *why*, or they wander through theory you can't actually use on a Monday morning. This book tries to do something different: connect the everyday work of defending systems to the reason that work exists in the first place—keeping a business running, its data trustworthy, and its people able to do their jobs.

That framing matters because security is not an end in itself. No organization exists to be secure; it exists to sell something, serve someone, or build something, and security is the discipline that lets it keep doing so without being robbed, halted, or embarrassed. The best security professionals are not the ones who say "no" most often. They are the ones who can look at a business goal, understand the risk around it, and find the path that achieves the goal *and* survives contact with a hostile internet.

This edition opens with concepts for thinking about strategy, risk, and the regulatory landscape of internet and network security, because tools deployed without judgment are just expensive noise. It then moves into genuine technical depth on the machinery you will actually configure and defend: how a firewall is built and deployed, how a next-generation firewall identifies applications and users and decides what to do with traffic, how and why encrypted traffic may be decrypted and what that means for security and privacy, how zero-trust and cloud-delivered security architectures fit together, and how logging and orchestration support real-world operations. The goal is to create a book you can learn from in practice and keep on the shelf as a working reference.

A note on tone and on vendors. The technologies described here are offered by many vendors under many brand names, and this book describes the concepts generically rather than endorsing any product. Where an idea is most commonly known by a particular name, that name is used so you can map it to what you will encounter in practice, but the understanding is meant to transfer across whatever platform you find yourself running. And throughout, the honest reality holds: defenders work with incomplete information, finite budgets, and adversaries who only have to be right once. What follows is not a promise of safety. It is a way of thinking and a body of practice that tilt the odds meaningfully in your favor.

Chapter 1: Thinking Like a Security Professional

IN THIS CHAPTER

Security as a business problem, not a technical one

The first instinct of many people new to security is to reach for tools... a new firewall, a fancier endpoint product, another dashboard. Tools matter, and we will spend much of this book on them, but they are the second move. The first move is always to understand what you are protecting and why.

Consider a small online retailer that asks you to "make us secure." That request is meaningless until you translate it into business terms. The company needs to take orders without the website going down. It needs customers' card details to stay confidential, because fraud is expensive and a breach would destroy the trust the business runs on. It needs its order database to stay accurate, because corrupted inventory or pricing costs real money. And it needs to keep operating even if a server fails or a laptop is stolen. None of those needs mentions a specific technology. They are outcomes, which is why its essential to stay available, keep data confidential, keep data accurate. Thinking like a security professional means starting from outcomes and working backward to controls, rather than starting from controls and hoping they add up to something useful.

This orientation toward outcomes is what separates a security engineer from a button-pusher. Anyone can follow a configuration guide. The professional understands what the configuration is *for*, which means they can tell when the guide is wrong for their situation, when a control is protecting nothing of value, and when an expensive purchase would buy less safety than a free configuration change. Tools are means; the business outcome is the end, and confusing the two is the most common and most expensive mistake in the field.

The CIA triad as an analytical tool

The classic model for these outcomes is the CIA triad: confidentiality, integrity, and availability. It is often taught as a definition to memorize, which sells it short; it is far more useful as a diagnostic lens you hold up to any system. Confidentiality asks who should be able to see this, and whether you are keeping everyone else out. Integrity asks whether the data is correct and unaltered, and whether you would know if someone changed it. Availability asks whether the people who need this can actually reach it when they need to.

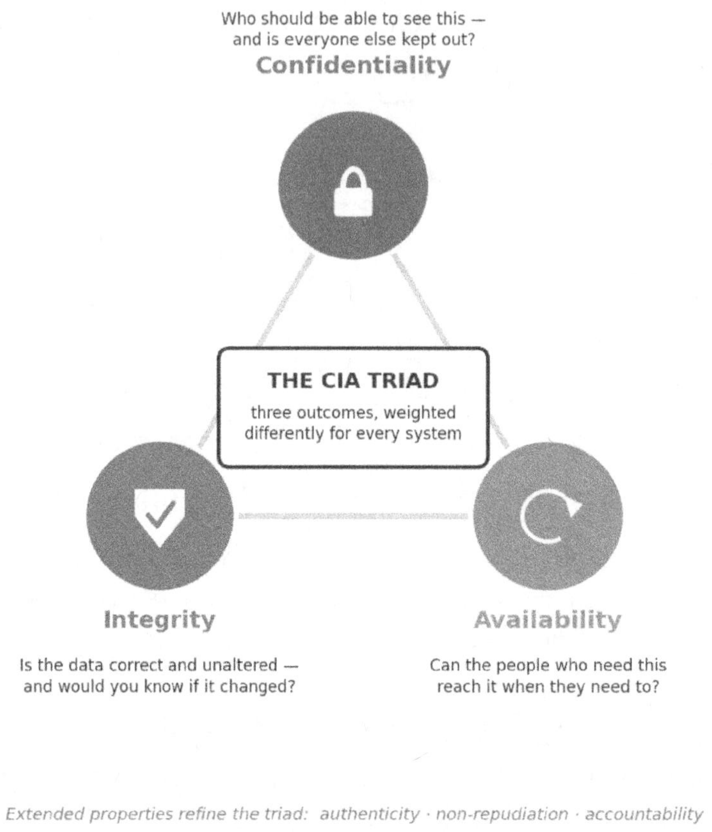

FIGURE 1.1 The CIA triad — confidentiality, integrity, and availability, with the extended properties that refine them.

The triad is powerful because different systems weight these three very differently, and that weighting drives every downstream decision. For a hospital, availability of patient records can be life-or-death, locking a doctor out during an emergency is itself a harm, which means a security control that improves confidentiality at the cost of availability might be exactly wrong there. For a defense contractor, confidentiality may dominate to the point that they would rather a system go offline than risk exposure, the opposite trade-off. For a financial ledger, integrity is paramount; a balance that is silently wrong is worse than one that is briefly unreachable, because the unreachable balance announces its own problem while the corrupted one does not. When you analyze a problem, ask which leg of the triad matters most here, because the answer tells you where to spend and which trade-offs are acceptable.

Some practitioners extend the triad with additional properties worth knowing. *Authenticity* asks whether something genuinely is what it claims to be, whether it's right sender, the right server, the right software, etc. *Non-repudiation* asks whether an actor can later deny having done something, which matters for audit trails and signed transactions. *Accountability* asks whether actions can be traced to the responsible party. These are not separate from the triad so much as refinements of it, and they become concrete when we discuss digital signatures, identity, and logging in later chapters.

A repeatable way to analyze a security problem

You will be handed vague, messy problems and asked for an answer. A structured approach keeps you from flailing, and the following sequence works for almost any security question. First, identify the asset and its value, what you are protecting and what it is worth if compromised, because the cost of protection should never exceed the value of the thing protected. Second, identify the threats: who or what might cause harm, including external attackers, malicious or careless insiders, and non-human threats such as hardware failures and natural disasters. Third, identify the vulnerabilities, where the asset is weak, whether in technology, process, or people. Fourth, assess the risk, which is roughly how likely a threat is to exploit a vulnerability combined with how bad it would be if it did. Fifth, weigh the options, which for any significant risk come down to four: reduce it with controls, transfer it through insurance or contract, accept it consciously, or avoid it by not doing the risky thing. Sixth, recommend, and be honest about the trade-offs, because every control costs something, money, performance, convenience, staff time, and a recommendation that ignores cost is not a recommendation but a wish.

This sequence is deliberately the same whether the question is enormous or trivial. “Should we allow staff to use personal phones for work?” runs through it: the asset is corporate data, the threats include device loss and malicious apps, the vulnerability is your limited control over a device you do not own, the risk depends on what data reaches the phone, and the options range from forbidding it, to requiring mobile device management, to accepting the risk for low-sensitivity roles. “How do we protect this new customer-facing application?” runs through the identical steps at larger scale. Internalizing the sequence means you are never staring at a blank page; you always know the next question to ask.

Controls: preventive, detective, corrective

It helps to classify controls by what they do in time relative to an incident, because a balanced defense needs all three kinds and many programs are lopsided. *Preventive* controls to stop bad things from happening with firewalls, encryption, access control, hardening. *Detective* controls to notice when something bad is happening or has happened with logging, monitoring, intrusion detection, and alerting. And *Corrective* controls to limit and repair the damage afterward through backups, incident response, failover. A program heavy on prevention but light on detection is the classic failure mode: it works until it doesn’t, and then the breach runs undetected for months because nobody was watching. Controls also divide along another axis into *technical* (implemented in technology), *administrative* (policies, procedures, training), and *physical* (locks, cameras, access badges). The strongest defenses combine categories, because an attacker who defeats one type often still faces another. A useful habit when reviewing any environment is to sketch this grid mentally and notice which cells are empty, since the empty cells are where surprises live.

FIGURE 1.2 Control types — every control acts at a moment in time and through a mechanism; balanced defense covers the grid.

Thinking like an attacker

A complement to thinking like a business professional is learning to think like an attacker, because you cannot defend well against a mind you have not tried to inhabit. The defender's natural posture is to protect what they have been told to protect, in the ways they have been taught, which leaves them blind to the paths an adversary would actually take, paths that often run through the seams between systems, the assumptions no one questioned, and the controls everyone trusts without testing. The attacker, by contrast, does not care about your organizational chart or your intended use of a system; they care only about what is reachable, what is weak, and what leads to what they want. Adopting that perspective, even briefly, transforms how you evaluate a defense. Instead of asking "have we followed the guide?" you ask "if I wanted to get to the customer database, how would I do it, and what is actually stopping me at each step?", a question that surfaces the real attack paths rather than the imagined ones.

Thinking like an attacker means assuming that anything reachable will be probed, that any input will be manipulated, that any trust will be abused, and that the adversary will chain together several small weaknesses that each seemed acceptable in isolation, because real breaches are rarely a single dramatic flaw and usually a sequence of modest ones that nobody connected. It means recognizing that attackers take the path of least resistance, so the defense that matters is not the strongest control but the weakest one on the route to something valuable, the unlocked side door beside the reinforced front gate. And it means internalizing the fundamental asymmetry that runs through this entire book—the defender must protect every path, while the attacker need only find one, which is precisely why defense in depth, least privilege, and the assumption of eventual breach are not pessimism but realism. This mindset is what penetration testing and red teaming, discussed later, formalize and hire out, but it is a habit every security professional should cultivate, holding it in balance with the business orientation that opened this chapter: one perspective tells you what is worth protecting and why, the other tells you how it will actually be attacked, and you need both to defend well.

Aligning recommendations with business objectives

A security recommendation that fights the business will lose, and it should. If your control makes a critical workflow so painful that staff route around it, you have created the illusion of security while pushing risk into the shadows where you cannot see it. The skill is to find controls that serve the objective rather than obstruct it. If the goal is "let our sales team close deals from anywhere," the answer is not "no remote access", it is remote access designed to be both usable and defensible, with strong authentication that does not require a fifteen-step login and device checks that happen quietly in the background. The objective and the security can be the same sentence. The best security is the one that is transparent to the end user, but still mitigates risk to the acceptable level that you intended.

This is also how you earn the standing to be heard. A professional known for finding the secure path to *yes* gets consulted early; the one known only for *no* gets routed around entirely, the worst outcome of all, because then risky decisions get made with no security input whatsoever. Security that is bolted on after a decision has been made is always weaker and more expensive than security that shaped the decision, so the political work of being seen as an enabler rather than an obstacle is not separate from the technical work; it is what makes the technical work possible.

Recommending solutions, products, and technologies

When it comes time to recommend a specific product, lead with the problem, not the product. A sound recommendation reads: here is the risk we are trying to reduce, here are the realistic options for reducing it, here is what each costs and what it buys us, and here is the one I recommend and why. The product is the conclusion of an argument, not the starting point.

Resist the gravitational pull of the shiny. Vendors are very good at making you feel that the latest category of tool is mandatory; sometimes it is, but often the larger gains come from doing the unglamorous basics well (patching, configuration, access control, backups, and more) which cost less and protect more than a marquee product bolted onto a shaky foundation. A theme you will hear throughout this book is that most breaches exploit known, preventable weaknesses rather than exotic wizardry, and your recommendations should reflect where the actual risk lives. We return to the discipline of product selection repeatedly, and most fully when discussing the firewall and operations platforms that anchor a modern defense, because those are the purchases where the gap between a thoughtful recommendation and a vendor-led one costs the most.

Chapter 2: Risk, Compliance, and Data Regulations

IN THIS CHAPTER

Security is the management of risk, not its elimination

If you take one idea from this book, take this: security is the management of risk, not the elimination of it. Perfect security is impossible, and even near-perfect security is usually unaffordable and would strangle the business and counteract the availability of your resources, the very thing you are aiming to protect. The professional's job is to bring risk down to a level the organization can knowingly live with, at a cost it can bear, and to be honest about what remains. There is no such thing as "secure" as a finished state, only "secure enough for these purposes, given these threats, at this cost, with these risks consciously accepted."

This reframing changes everything downstream. It means there is no finished state to reach and rest in, only a posture to maintain as the world shifts around you. It means your recommendations are always arguments about trade-offs rather than absolute pronouncements, which is why the professional who says "here is the risk we are choosing to accept, and here is why" is being more rigorous, not less, than the one who claims to have made everything safe. And it means that the measure of a security program is not whether it was ever breached, but whether the risks it carried were understood, prioritized, and consciously chosen.

A workable definition: risk is the potential for loss or harm when a threat exploits a vulnerability, considered in terms of how likely that is and how much it would hurt. Those two dimensions, likelihood and impact, are what you are always weighing. A trivially exploitable flaw that only exposes the lunch menu is high-likelihood, low-impact and probably not worth much effort; a flaw that is hard to exploit but would expose every customer's financial records is low-likelihood, high-impact and very much worth attention. Most decisions live in the messy middle, and your job is to rank them so finite resources go to the risks that matter most because you will never have the budget to address every risk, and risk assessment is precisely what lets you spend your limited defense where it does the most good rather than spreading it evenly and thinly across everything, which is how organizations end up with elaborate protection on trivia and gaping holes around their crown jewels.

Threats, vulnerabilities, and the difference between them

Clear thinking about risk depends on not confusing its components. A *threat* is any potential cause of harm, whether it comes from a ransomware crew, a careless employee, or a flood. A *vulnerability* is any weakness that a threat could exploit, such as an unpatched server, a reused password, or a single power supply with no backup. A *risk* is what emerges when a threat meets a matching vulnerability in a way that could hurt something valuable. The distinction is practical, not academic, because your controls act on different parts of it. You usually cannot eliminate threats. You do not control whether ransomware crews exist, but you can reduce vulnerabilities, which is most of defensive work, and you can reduce impact, which is the work of backups, segmentation, and incident response. A threat with no matching vulnerability is not a risk to you, and a vulnerability that no threat can reach is a low priority. Mapping the two against each other is how you find the genuine risks hiding among the noise of every possible bad thing.

Risk assumptions: being explicit about what you believe

Every risk judgment rests on beliefs about the world: how capable your adversaries are, how valuable your data is to someone else, how likely a given failure is, how quickly you could recover. These beliefs are assumptions, and the danger is leaving them unstated, because unstated assumptions cannot be challenged or revisited. Make them explicit and write them down "we are assuming our primary threat is financially motivated criminals using commodity tools, not a nation-state"; "we are assuming a day of downtime costs roughly this much"; "we are assuming our backups are good, which we have not tested in six months." The moment an assumption is on paper, others can disagree with it and improve it, and you can notice when reality has drifted from it.

Different assumptions lead to entirely different and entirely correct postures. A neighborhood bakery and a cryptocurrency exchange both handle money, but their realistic adversaries, the value of what they hold, and the consequences of compromise differ by orders of magnitude. A practice that is prudent for the exchange would bankrupt the bakery in both money and friction, and one adequate for the bakery would be negligent for the exchange. Best practices are not universal; they are relative to a threat model and a set of assumptions. When someone asks for "best practices," the honest first response is "best practices for what threat model, protecting what, against whom?", not pedantry but the only way to give an answer that is actually right rather than merely conventional.

Qualitative and quantitative assessment

There are two broad styles of assessing risk, and mature programs use both. Qualitative assessment uses judgment-based categories (high, medium, or low) often arranged on a grid of likelihood against impact. It is fast, communicable to non-experts, and good enough for most prioritization; its weakness is that "high" means different things to different people and the categories can imply a false precision. Quantitative assessment attaches numbers, usually money estimating how much a single occurrence would cost and how often it is expected per year, then multiplying to express an expected annual cost. Its appeal is that it speaks the language of executives, as money usually runs the business, and lets you compare a security spend directly against the loss it prevents; its catch is that the inputs are often educated guesses dressed up as figures, and a precise-looking number built on shaky estimates can mislead more than an honest "high." Use quantitative methods where you have real data and qualitative methods everywhere else, and never let a decimal point fool you into trusting a guess.

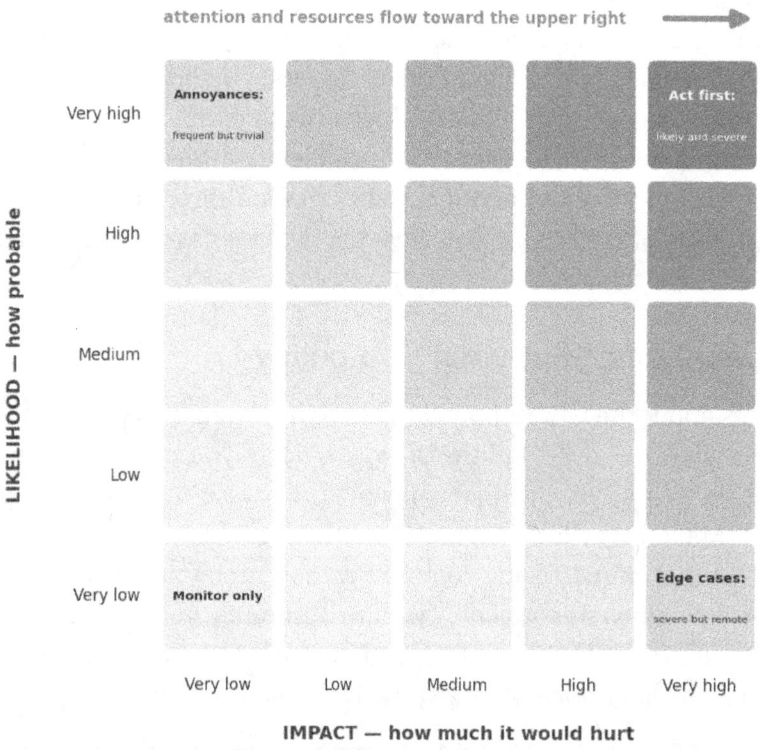

FIGURE 2.1 A qualitative risk matrix — likelihood against impact, with attention and resources flowing toward the upper right.

The four ways to treat a risk

Once you have assessed a risk you have four fundamental responses, and almost every real decision blends them. You can *mitigate* it to reduce the likelihood or impact with controls, which is the bulk of security work and rarely takes a risk to zero. You can *transfer* it to shift financial consequence to someone else through insurance or a contract clause, while remembering that you can transfer the financial pain but rarely the reputational pain, since customers blame you, not your insurer. You can *accept* it and decide consciously that further reduction costs more than it is worth, which is legitimate and necessary so long as it is conscious and documented; the same risk left unaddressed because nobody noticed is negligence, and the only difference between sound risk acceptance and dangerous neglect is whether anyone made the decision on purpose. Or you can *avoid* it to eliminate the risk by not doing the risky activity at all, the most complete response and often the most overlooked, because it requires the discipline to forgo something that looked appealing.

Frameworks, control catalogs, and certifications: three distinct components of security governance

You do not have to invent risk management from scratch. A large ecosystem of published guidance already exists to help organizations structure security programs and make consistent decisions. However, that ecosystem is frequently misunderstood because several fundamentally different concepts are often grouped together under broad terms such as "framework" or "compliance." As a result, organizations sometimes apply the wrong tool to the problem at hand or mistakenly treat one category as a substitute for another when they serve entirely different purposes.

Before examining specific examples, it is useful to distinguish among three categories: risk-management frameworks, control catalogs, and certifications or validations. Once these distinctions are clear, the broader security landscape becomes much easier to navigate.

A risk-management framework explains how to organize and operate a security program. It defines processes, sequencing, governance, and decision-making activities, but it does not by itself provide the detailed technical controls to implement. A control catalog serves the complementary role: it provides the specific safeguards, configurations, and security controls that organizations may choose to implement, but it does not prescribe the overall process for managing the program that selects and applies those controls.

Certifications and validations represent a third category entirely. Rather than providing guidance, they provide independent verification that an organization, system, or product meets a defined set of requirements. In other words, frameworks and control catalogs are resources you use internally to build and manage security programs, whereas certifications and validations are external attestations that demonstrate compliance with a particular standard or benchmark.

These categories answer different questions and are used at different stages of security governance. The sections that follow examine each in turn before concluding with a comparative table that places them side by side.

Risk-management frameworks

The best-known of these is the *NIST Cybersecurity Framework*, the CSF, which organizes security into a small set of high-level functions and is prized precisely because it is not bogged down in technical detail. It is a way to structure a program and, just as importantly, to talk about it with leadership who do not speak in control numbers. In its 2.0 revision the framework defines six functions: *Govern*, added in that revision to make explicit that security must be steered by organizational governance and risk decisions, alongside the original five of *Identify*, *Protect*, *Detect*, *Respond*, and *Recover*. The CSF tells you the outcomes to pursue; it deliberately leaves the choice of specific controls to you, which is what makes it adaptable across organizations of wildly different size and risk. This book's later chapters implicitly follow its shape.

Where the CSF is a flexible organizing model, the *NIST Risk Management Framework*, the RMF, is a formal, prescriptive *process*, the step-by-step lifecycle that United States federal systems must follow, and that many others borrow. It runs through a defined sequence: prepare, categorize the system by impact, select controls, implement them, assess that they work, authorize the system to operate by having a responsible official formally accept the residual risk, and then continuously monitor. The RMF is more rigid and more detailed than the CSF because it exists to produce a specific outcome, a defensible authorization decision for a particular system rather than to organize a whole program at a high level.

A third entry needs a careful word because it wears two hats and that is part of what confuses people. *ISO/IEC 27001* is, in this section, a risk-management framework: it is the international standard defining the requirements for an *information security management system*, centered on a documented risk assessment and a Statement of Applicability explaining which controls the organization adopted and why. But ISO 27001 is also the thing an organization gets *certified against*, and in that sense it reappears in the certifications section below. Holding both faces in mind at once is the key: the standard is a framework you build your program around, and certification is the independent verification that you did so, and the same name covers both.

Finally, not every framework spans an entire program; some target a particular problem domain. *NIST SP 800-207* is the canonical reference architecture for *zero trust*, the model developed in the architecture chapter, giving structured guidance for building toward never-trust-always-verify rather than leaving it a slogan. Where 800-207 defines *what* zero trust is, the *CISA Zero Trust Maturity Model* helps an organization work out *where it currently stands and how to progress*, and the two are complementary rather than competing: the maturity model is built on the same concept the architecture defines. It organizes the journey across five pillars: identity, devices, networks, applications and workloads, and data. Underpinned by cross-cutting capabilities in visibility and analytics, automation and orchestration, and governance, CISA Zero Trust Maturity Model grades each pillar through maturity stages running from traditional, through initial and advanced, to optimal. This lets an organization assess each pillar honestly, see which are lagging, and plan the incremental path that the architecture chapter insists zero trust must be, rather than treating it as a single overnight transformation. The *NIST AI Risk Management Framework*, the AI RMF, addresses the distinctive risks of artificial-intelligence systems through its own set of functions (govern, map, measure, and manage) and is the natural companion to the AI chapter later in this book, supplying the structured approach that chapter's discussion of AI risk otherwise only gestures at. These domain frameworks do not replace the general ones; they plug into the broader program wherever their particular problem space is in play.

Control catalogs

If frameworks tell you how to run the program, *control catalogs* are the menu of specific controls the program selects from the detailed list of what to actually do. The most comprehensive is *NIST SP 800-53*, an extensive catalog of security and privacy controls organized into families, which also defines *baselines*, predefined starting sets of controls corresponding to low, moderate, and high impact systems, so that you are not choosing from the whole catalog blindly but tailoring a sensible default. Its rough international counterpart is *ISO/IEC 27002*, the control guidance that accompanies the ISO 27001 standard, elaborating the controls that 27001 lists. And the *CIS Controls* offer a deliberately prioritized, opinionated set of defensive actions arranged into implementation groups, valued precisely because they tell a resource-constrained organization what to do *first* rather than presenting an undifferentiated list, an embodiment of the risk-prioritization thinking this chapter has urged throughout. A catalog is not a program and not a certificate; it is the well-stocked shelf from which the framework's process tells you what to take.

How they fit together: the NIST pipeline, end to end

These pieces are often cited as a bewildering string of numbers, but the core NIST documents form a coherent assembly line, and walking it from start to finish shows exactly how framework, standard, and catalog interlock which is the clearest way to dissolve the confusion. Suppose you must secure a system that holds customer records.

It begins with *FIPS 199*, the standard for security categorization, which asks you to rate the potential impact (low, moderate, or high) of a loss of each of confidentiality, integrity, and availability for the information and the system. Our customer records might rate confidentiality as moderate, integrity as moderate, and availability as low; the system then takes the *high-water mark* across these, so it is categorized as a moderate-impact system overall. That single categorization is the input that drives everything downstream, which is why getting it right matters.

Next, *FIPS 200* establishes the minimum security requirements for the system and directs you, based on that impact level, to select an appropriate set of controls. It points you to the catalog to do so. You therefore turn to *NIST SP 800-53*, draw the *moderate* baseline of controls that corresponds to the categorization, and then *tailor* it to your actual system, adding controls where your risk demands and removing or adjusting others with documented justification. Categorization fed selection; selection drew from the catalog.

Wrapping all of this is the *Risk Management Framework*, SP 800-37, the process introduced above: it is the lifecycle within which categorization (using FIPS 199), selection (using 800-53), implementation, assessment, authorization, and continuous monitoring all happen in order. The RMF is the conveyor belt; FIPS 199, FIPS 200, and 800-53 are stations along it. And the *CSF* sits above the whole apparatus at the program and governance level: its six functions are the high-level outcomes and the common language for prioritizing and for talking to leadership, while the RMF pipeline is the detailed machinery for authorizing an individual system. Put plainly, the CSF tells an executive what the organization is trying to achieve; the RMF pipeline tells an engineer exactly which controls to put on this particular system and how to prove they work. Then the domain frameworks, like NIST 800-207 or AI RMF, slot in to shape the controls when the system is built that focuses on guidance.. Seeing it as a pipeline rather than a pile is the whole point: each piece hands off to the next, categorize to select to implement to assess to authorize to monitor, with governance wrapping the entire flow.

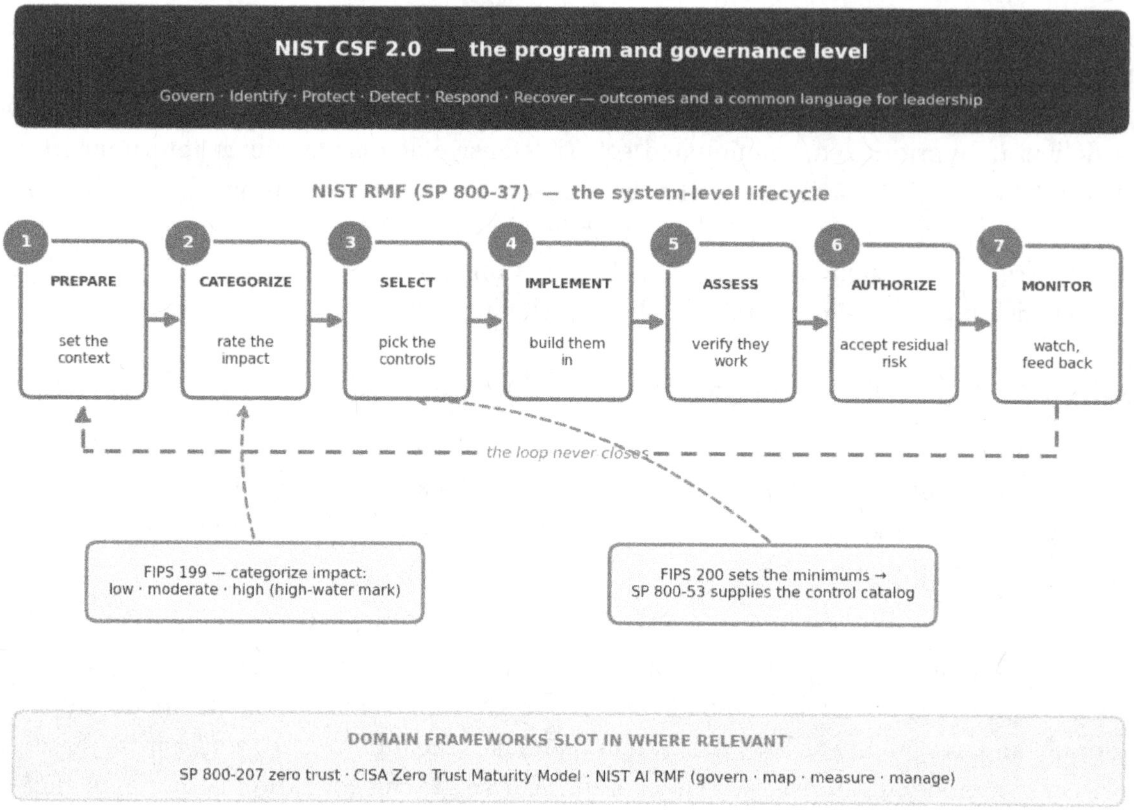

FIGURE 2.2 The NIST pipeline — FIPS 199 categorization through SP 800-53 control selection, run as the RMF lifecycle beneath the CSF.

Certifications and validations

The third category is genuinely different from the frameworks and catalogs above, because it produces an independent, external verification that a specific thing meets a defined bar rather than internal guidance you apply yourself. Three are worth distinguishing precisely, because they too are routinely confused.

ISO/IEC 27001 certification is the verification face of the standard introduced earlier: an accredited auditor examines an organization's information security management system against the 27001 requirements and issues a pass/fail certificate, attesting to how the company manages security as a discipline rather than to any single piece of technology. *SOC 2* is closely related in purpose but different in form: it is an *attestation*, a report written by auditors against a defined set of trust criteria describing an organization's controls and how they actually performed, delivered as a point-in-time report or, more rigorously, as a report covering a period of operation, with no pass/fail certificate attached. When someone says "send me your audit," they almost always mean the SOC 2 report. Both are broad, organizational trust signals, and crucially a company can hold either while still using ordinary, unvalidated encryption, because both let the organization justify its own choices against its own risk assessment.

FIPS 140-3 is a different animal entirely, and placing it in this category rather than among the frameworks is exactly the correction this section makes. It is a *validation*, not a framework: it verifies that a specific *cryptographic module* (the bounded component that actually performs encryption and guards keys) meets the standard, through laboratory testing, producing a validation certificate on a public government list. Its international technical equivalent is ISO/IEC 19790, on which FIPS 140-3 is built, though United States government buyers usually still demand the FIPS certificate by name. The distinction that matters for drafting requirements is now clean: FIPS 140-3 verifies *the cryptography itself*, while ISO 27001 or SOC 2 verifies *the program around it*. They are complementary, not interchangeable, which is why a careful contract sometimes asks for more than one, as each answers a different question. Conflating them is precisely the error this restructured section is meant to retire.

The landscape at a glance

The table below maps the items above to their categories so the distinctions stay clear at a glance.

TABLE 2.1 The standards landscape at a glance

Name	Category	What it is	What it produces or verifies
NIST CSF 2.0	Risk-management framework	High-level program outcomes across six functions: Govern, Identify, Protect, Detect, Respond, Recover	A common structure and language for a program; no certificate
NIST RMF (SP 800-37)	Risk-management process	The step-by-step categorize-to-authorize lifecycle for a system	An authorization decision (authority to operate)
ISO/IEC 27001 (standard)	Risk-management framework	Requirements for an information security management system	The basis a program is built and audited against
NIST SP 800-207	Domain framework (zero trust)	Reference architecture for zero trust	Design guidance, not a certificate
CISA Zero Trust Maturity Model	Domain framework (zero trust maturity)	Maturity model across five pillars, graded through staged progress	A self-assessment and incremental roadmap; no certificate
NIST AI RMF	Domain framework (AI risk)	Approach to governing AI risk: Govern, Map, Measure, Manage	Governance guidance, not a certificate
NIST SP 800-53	Control catalog	Catalog of security and privacy controls with impact baselines	A menu of controls to select and tailor
ISO/IEC 27002	Control catalog	Control guidance accompanying ISO 27001	A menu of controls to select
CIS Controls	Control catalog (prioritized)	A prioritized set of defensive actions in implementation groups	A ranked list of what to do first
FIPS 199 / FIPS 200	Standards (categorization and minimums)	Categorize system impact, then set minimum requirements	The impact level that drives control selection
ISO/IEC 27001 certification	Certification	Accredited audit of an ISMS against the 27001 standard	A pass/fail certificate
SOC 2	Attestation	Auditor's report on controls against trust criteria	An attestation report (point-in-time or over a period)
FIPS 140-3	Validation	Lab testing of a cryptographic module (≈ ISO/IEC 19790)	A validation certificate on the public NIST list

Whichever of these you use, the closing caution is the same: they are scaffolding, not scripture. They keep you from forgetting whole categories of risk and give you a common language with auditors, regulators, and leadership, but they never replace judgment about your specific organization, and a program that follows a framework to the letter while ignoring its own peculiar risks has confused the map for the territory.

The data-regulation landscape

Risk does not exist in a legal vacuum. A growing patchwork of laws and standards dictates how organizations must handle different categories of data, and noncompliance is itself a major source of risk. Regulatory violations can lead to fines, lawsuits, contractual penalties, and mandatory breach notifications. Security professionals do not need to be lawyers, but they do need enough familiarity with the regulatory landscape to recognize when a law or standard applies and to help design controls that satisfy it. The legal specifics belong to counsel, and nothing here should be interpreted as legal advice.

GDPR and the global privacy model

The most influential modern privacy regime is the European Union's General Data Protection Regulation (GDPR). GDPR governs the personal data of individuals in the EU and applies extraterritorially to organizations outside Europe that process such data. It grants individuals rights over their information, including rights of access and erasure, requires organizations to establish a lawful basis for processing data, and mandates breach notification.

The regulation's financial penalties are substantial enough to command executive and board-level attention, and its influence extends far beyond Europe. Many later privacy laws around the world adopted concepts, terminology, and structures first popularized by GDPR.

The United States' sector-and-state approach

The United States does not have a single comprehensive national privacy law. Instead, it relies on a combination of sector-specific federal laws and state-level regulations.

The California Consumer Privacy Act (CCPA) and the later California Privacy Rights Act (CPRA) have become a de facto national baseline for many organizations because companies often choose to apply California standards broadly rather than maintain separate compliance models by state. Other states have increasingly enacted similar laws.

Several federal laws regulate specific categories of sensitive data. HIPAA governs protected health information in healthcare environments and imposes safeguards on organizations that handle it. The Gramm-Leach-Bliley Act (GLBA) applies to financial institutions, while FERPA protects student education records. Sarbanes-Oxley (SOX), although primarily focused on financial reporting and corporate governance, also carries important security implications because it requires organizations to maintain reliable controls over financial systems and records.

Outside the United States, countries including Canada, Brazil, and the United Kingdom maintain their own privacy and data-protection regimes. The overall trend worldwide is unmistakable: regulation is expanding rather than shrinking.

PCI DSS: a contractual standard with regulatory force

One important framework deserves separate treatment: the Payment Card Industry Data Security Standard (PCI DSS). PCI DSS is not a law. Instead, it is a contractual standard imposed by the major payment-card brands on organizations that process, store, or transmit cardholder data.

In practice, however, PCI DSS often functions much like a regulation because compliance is required to participate in the payment-card ecosystem. Unlike many legal frameworks, PCI DSS is highly prescriptive. It mandates specific technical and operational controls, including strong cryptography, network segmentation, access control, logging, and regular security testing.

Its segmentation requirements in particular have had a major influence on real-world network architecture because organizations frequently isolate cardholder-data environments from the rest of their infrastructure to reduce compliance scope and risk exposure.

Cross-cutting issues: residency, sovereignty, and breach notification

Two broader concepts cut across nearly all modern data-regulation regimes.

The first is data residency and data sovereignty. These concepts concern where data is physically stored and which country's laws therefore govern it. This becomes especially important in cloud environments, where data may be distributed across multiple geographic regions. Decisions about cloud architecture, data replication, and SASE deployments can therefore carry legal as well as technical implications.

The second is breach notification. Most modern privacy and security regimes impose requirements governing how organizations must respond to data breaches, including notification timelines and disclosure obligations. As a result, incident response is not purely a technical function. Legal counsel, executive leadership, communications teams, and compliance personnel often need to be involved from the earliest stages of a significant incident.

Compliance versus security

The practical takeaway is straightforward: organizations must understand what data they hold, how sensitive it is, and which legal or contractual obligations apply to it. They must also build and document controls capable of satisfying those obligations.

At the same time, compliance should be treated as a minimum baseline rather than the ultimate goal. Compliance and security overlap heavily, but they are not the same thing. An organization can be fully compliant and still be insecure if it treats regulatory checklists as the entirety of security rather than as the minimum standard required.

TABLE 2.2 Major data regulations at a glance

Regulation	Who and what it covers	Character and consequences
GDPR (EU)	Personal data of individuals in the EU; applies extraterritorially to organizations outside Europe that process such data	Grants individuals rights over their data; penalties substantial enough to command executive and board-level attention; the model many later privacy laws adopted
CCPA / CPRA (California)	California consumers' personal data	A de facto national baseline that companies often apply from California's broadly framed privacy standards rather than maintaining separate compliance models by state
HIPAA (US)	Protected health information in healthcare environments	Imposes safeguards on organizations that handle health data
GLBA (US)	Financial institutions	Sector-specific federal privacy and safeguard requirements
FERPA (US)	Student education records	Protects the privacy of education records
SOX (US)	Public-company financial reporting and corporate governance	Requires reliable controls over financial systems and records, carrying security implications
PCI DSS (contractual)	Organizations that process, store, or transmit cardholder data	A highly prescriptive contractual standard imposed by the payment-card brands; segmentation requirements shape real network architecture
Other national regimes	Canada, Brazil, the United Kingdom, and others	The worldwide trend is unmistakable: regulation is expanding rather than shrinking
Cross-cutting: residency and sovereignty	Where data is physically stored and which country's laws govern it	Cloud architecture, data replication, and SASE decisions carry legal as well as technical implications
Cross-cutting: breach notification	How organizations must respond to breaches	Notification timelines and disclosure obligations make incident response a legal and communications function, not purely a technical one

Chapter 3: Assets, Threats, and the Anatomy of an Attack

IN THIS CHAPTER

You cannot defend what you cannot see

There is an old and reliable truth in security: the asset you forget about is the one that gets you breached. Attackers are diligent about mapping your systems; they will find the forgotten test server, the abandoned cloud account, the device a contractor plugged in two years ago and nobody removed. If your inventory is worse than the attacker's map of you, you are defending blind. So the foundation of protection is unglamorous: a current, accurate inventory of your hardware, your software and its versions, and your data: where it lives, how sensitive it is, who can reach it, and where it flows. Many organizations discover during their first serious inventory that they have far more attack surface than they believed, and that a meaningful fraction of it is unmanaged, which is to say invisible to every control they have bought.

The attack surface is the sum of all the points where an attacker could try to get in or get data out: every open port, running service, user account, internet-facing application, exposed management interface, and third-party integration. The single most reliable way to improve security is to make this surface smaller. A service that is not running cannot be exploited; an account that does not exist cannot be compromised; a port that is closed cannot be scanned and attacked; software that is not installed has no vulnerabilities to patch. Much of hardening, which we treat shortly, is simply the disciplined removal of things you do not need so that there is less to defend and less to go wrong. Attack-surface reduction is the rare security activity that simultaneously improves security, lowers cost, and simplifies operations, which is why it should be the first thing you reach for and the last thing you economize on.

Not all data deserves equal protection, and treating it as if it does wastes resources on the trivial while underprotecting the critical. Data classification sorts information into tiers by how much harm its exposure or loss would cause: public, internal, confidential, restricted, or some similar scheme. Classification drives concrete decisions throughout the rest of this book: restricted data warrants strong encryption, tight access control, careful logging, decryption-and-inspection of the traffic carrying it, and the data-loss-prevention measures of a later chapter, while public data needs integrity protection but little confidentiality. Getting classification right means your strongest, most expensive controls land on the data that would hurt most if lost—the risk-prioritization logic of the previous chapter applied to information itself—and it is also the foundation on which data loss prevention and traffic inspection later depend, because a tool can only protect what it has been taught to recognize as valuable.

The threat actors, honestly

To protect assets you have to understand who you are protecting them from, and it pays to be specific rather than to imagine a generic hooded figure. The most common adversary by far is the financially motivated criminal: the operators behind ransomware, banking fraud, business email compromise, and data theft for resale. They are largely opportunistic and economically rational, hunting easy targets and known weaknesses because their business model depends on efficiency rather than artistry. This is genuinely good news for defenders: solid basics deter most of them, and they move on to softer targets, much as a burglar passes the house with the alarm sign for the one without. A more capable tier comprises organized cybercrime groups operating like businesses, with specialization, tooling, and even customer support for their ransomware victims. At the far end sit nation-state actors and advanced persistent threats, well-resourced, patient, and willing to develop custom capabilities, pursuing espionage or strategic sabotage rather than quick money. Most organizations are not realistic targets for that tier, which is exactly why your risk assumptions should be honest about who actually wants to hurt you; defending a small retailer as though it faced a nation-state wastes money that should go to the criminal threat it actually faces. Other actors round out the picture: hacktivists motivated by ideology, insiders discussed below, and the merely curious or reckless.

Internal threats come from inside the trust boundary and are easy to underrate because they do not fit the dramatic image. The malicious insider deliberately steals data, sabotages systems, or sells access, often using legitimate credentials, which makes them dangerous and hard to catch because their actions can look authorized. Far more common is the negligent insider: the well-meaning employee who clicks the phishing link, misconfigures the cloud storage, emails a spreadsheet to the wrong person, reuses a password, or loses a laptop. Most internal incidents are mistakes, not malice, which is why training and good defaults matter as much as monitoring, and why a punitive culture that makes people hide their mistakes is itself a security weakness.

The anatomy of an attack: the kill chain

Real attacks are usually not a single dramatic event but a sequence of stages, and understanding the sequence shows you where you can intervene. A widely used model breaks an intrusion into phases that, while no real attack follows them perfectly, give a shared vocabulary and a map of opportunities to detect and disrupt. Reconnaissance is the attacker learning about your people, your technology, your exposed services, and often using nothing more than public information and a port scan. Weaponization and delivery is preparing the malicious payload and getting it to you, most often through a phishing email, a malicious website, a compromised supplier, or an exposed and vulnerable service. Exploitation is the moment the payload runs or the vulnerability is triggered, giving the attacker their first foothold. Installation establishes persistence so the attacker survives a reboot or a password change. Command and control is the attacker establishing a channel to operate the compromised system remotely, often disguised as ordinary traffic. And actions on objectives is the attacker finally doing what they came to do: stealing data, deploying ransomware, committing fraud, or destroying systems.

The defensive insight from this model is liberating: you do not have to stop every stage, you only have to break the chain at any single point. An attacker who is detected and stopped during command and control has been defeated even though reconnaissance, delivery, exploitation, and installation all succeeded. This is the deep justification for defense in depth and it reframes detection from a consolation prize into a primary objective, because catching an attack mid-sequence stops it just as surely as preventing it would have.

The kill chain is a high-level, roughly linear story of an intrusion, which is exactly what makes it useful for reasoning about where to intervene, but its broad stages are too coarse to drive detection on their own, because knowing that an attacker eventually "moves laterally" does not tell you what to look for. The framework that supplies that missing granularity, and the one you will encounter constantly in practice, is MITRE ATT&CK: a large, freely available knowledge base of adversary tactics and techniques drawn from real-world observed attacks and maintained by the MITRE organization. It is worth being precise about what kind of thing ATT&CK is, because it is easily confused with the program frameworks and control catalogs of the risk chapter and it is neither. ATT&CK is descriptive and documents what adversaries actually do. It is, in effect, a fourth kind of reference altogether: a threat knowledge base, a structured encyclopedia of attacker behavior.

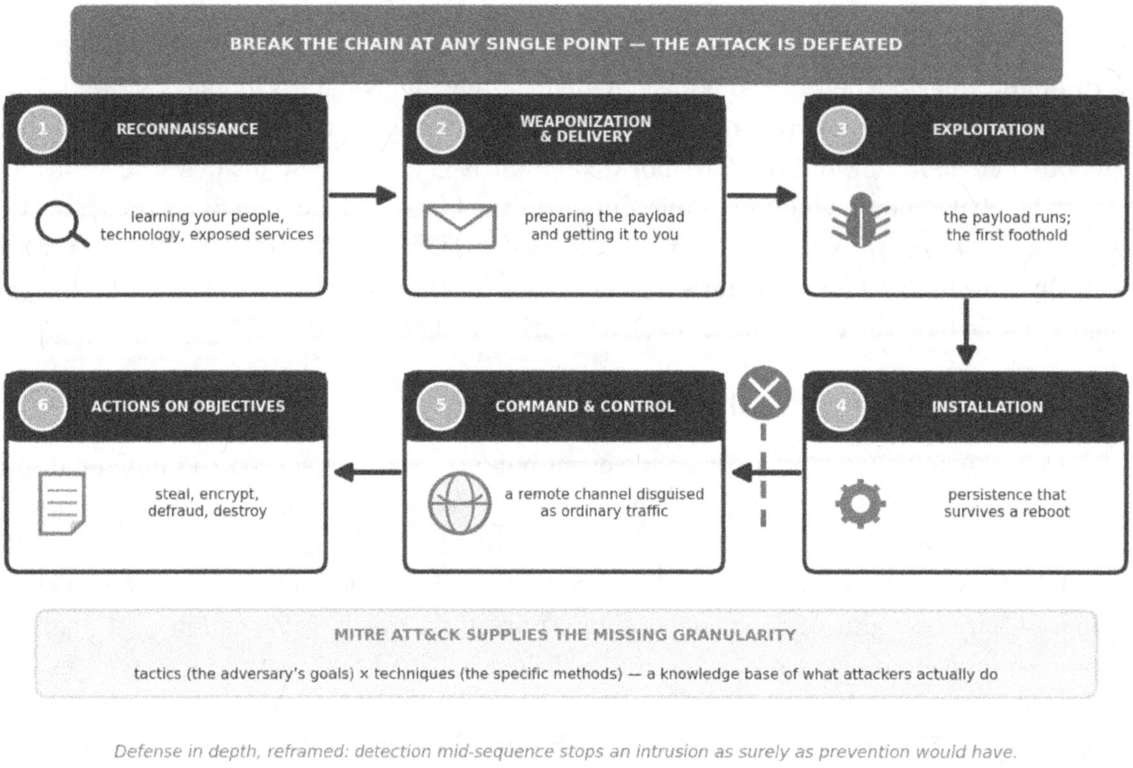

FIGURE 3.1 The kill chain — an intrusion as a sequence of stages; breaking any link breaks the attack.

ATT&CK is organized as a matrix along two dimensions. The tactics which are the adversary's goals and read like a more detailed, less strictly ordered version of the kill chain's stages: reconnaissance, initial access, execution, persistence, privilege escalation, defense evasion, credential access, discovery, lateral movement, collection, command and control, exfiltration, and impact, among others. Under each tactic sit the techniques of how, the specific methods adversaries use to achieve that goal. Beneath many techniques also sits a still more granular sub-techniques, so that "credential access" resolves into concrete, recognizable behaviors an attacker might perform and a defender might detect. Because every technique is grounded in behavior seen in actual intrusions and is documented with the procedures real adversary groups have used to carry it out, ATT&CK grounds defense in what attackers demonstrably do rather than in what defenders imagine they might.

The practical uses of ATT&CK are what make it so pervasive, and all of them connect directly to the detection and operations work of the later chapters. The central use is coverage mapping, or gap analysis: a detection team works across the matrix asking, for each technique an adversary might plausibly use against them, whether they could actually detect it, and where the answer is no, that gap becomes a prioritized piece of work, turning a vague worry about "are we catching attacks?" into a concrete, technique-by-technique inventory of what is and is not covered. ATT&CK also gives the whole field a common vocabulary: threat-intelligence reports describe adversary groups in terms of the techniques they favor, incident responders map what they observed to specific techniques, and red teams use the matrix to emulate a realistic adversary by reproducing the techniques a particular group is known to use, so that the defense is tested against how real attackers behave rather than against a generic checklist. This approach, building and measuring defenses around documented adversary behavior, is often called threat-informed defense, and it is the natural deepening of the kill chain introduced above: the kill chain tells you that breaking the sequence anywhere defeats the attack, and ATT&CK tells you, in actionable detail, exactly which behaviors to watch for at each step. You do not need to memorize the matrix, but knowing it exists, knowing what kind of reference it is, and using it to find and close the gaps in your detection is a clear mark of operational maturity.

Lateral movement and why the inside matters

Two stages of the sequence deserve emphasis because they are where flat, trusting networks fail catastrophically. Privilege escalation is the attacker climbing from the ordinary account they first compromised toward administrative control, exploiting misconfigurations, unpatched flaws, or harvested credentials. Lateral movement is the attacker spreading from the first machine toward the systems that actually hold what they want, hopping from host to host using stolen credentials and trusted internal pathways. These two stages are the reason that getting a foothold is rarely the same as achieving the objective, and they are precisely what segmentation, microsegmentation, least privilege, and internal monitoring are designed to obstruct. An attacker who lands on a receptionist's workstation has gained little if that workstation can reach almost nothing else and every attempt to expand is blocked and logged; the same foothold on a flat network where everything trusts everything is a catastrophe. Much of the modern architecture in later chapters exists to ensure that the inevitable initial compromise stays small.

Social engineering and the human attack surface

Phishing, discussed below in its email form, is one expression of a broader and older art: social engineering, the manipulation of people into taking actions or divulging information that compromises security. It deserves separate attention because it bypasses technology entirely, targeting the human judgment that no patch can fix, and because it is involved in a remarkable share of real breaches. Social engineering works by exploiting reliable features of human psychology rather than flaws in software. Authority makes people comply with apparent superiors or officials, which is why an attacker impersonates an executive or the IT department. Urgency short-circuits careful thought, which is why the message insists something must be done right now or terrible consequences follow. Reciprocity and helpfulness exploit the natural desire to assist, which is why an attacker poses as a confused colleague needing a small favor. Familiarity and trust are manufactured through research, so that the approach references real names, projects, and details that make the imposter credible.

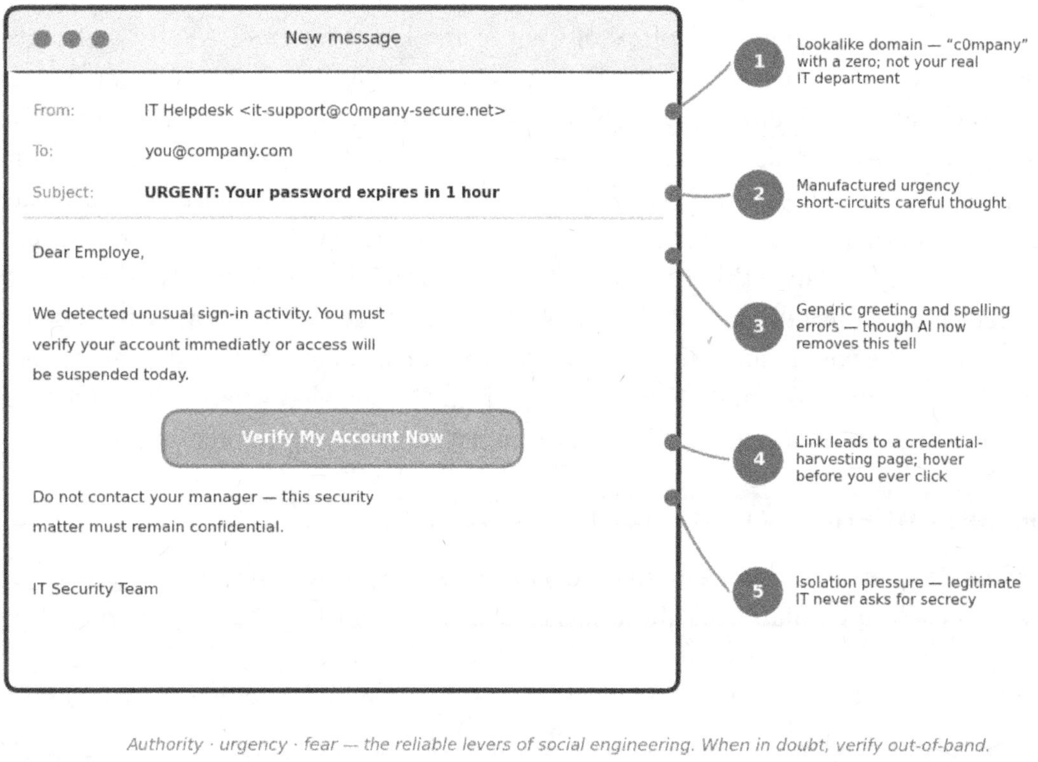

FIGURE 3.2 Anatomy of a phishing email — the telltale signs, annotated.

The techniques extend well beyond email. Pretexting invents a plausible scenario (e.g. a vendor calling about an invoice, a new employee needing access) to extract information or action over the phone or in person. Baiting leaves tempting bait, such as a malicious drive labeled to provoke curiosity, where a target will find and use it. Tailgating simply follows an authorized person through a secure door, exploiting politeness. Business email compromise, one of the costliest categories of fraud, uses a compromised or spoofed executive account to direct an employee to wire money or change payment details, combining technical access with social manipulation. The unifying defense is the same blend the threats discussion keeps returning to: technical controls that reduce what a fooled human can give away, above all phishing-resistant authentication and out-of-band verification of unusual requests, paired with a culture in which people feel safe questioning an authoritative-sounding demand and reporting their own mistakes. You cannot patch people, but you can build processes that hold even when a person is deceived, and that is what defending the human attack surface actually means.

The ransomware ecosystem

Ransomware deserves a closer look than its place in the malware taxonomy suggests, because it has become the defining criminal threat of the era and because understanding how it operates as a business sharpens the defense. Modern ransomware is rarely the work of a lone author; it is an industry with specialization and supply chains of its own. Some groups develop the ransomware and rent it to others as a service, taking a cut of the proceeds, which means a single capable development team can power attacks by many less-skilled affiliates. Initial-access brokers specialize in breaking into organizations and selling that access to ransomware operators, turning the foothold into a commodity. This division of labor is why the threat is so pervasive: each participant does one thing well, and the whole ecosystem scales.

A modern ransomware attack typically unfolds over the kill chain described above rather than striking instantly. The attackers gain access, often through phishing, stolen credentials, or an unpatched internet-facing service; they establish persistence and escalate privileges; they move laterally to understand and reach as much of the environment as possible; and, crucially, before encrypting anything, they frequently steal large volumes of sensitive data and identify and destroy or encrypt the backups, because backups are the victim's escape from paying. Only then do they trigger the encryption. This sequence drives the defense. The data theft means that even a flawless backup no longer fully neutralizes the threat, because the attackers add extortion, threatening to publish the stolen data unless paid, a pressure that a backup cannot relieve. The targeting of backups means that backups must be isolated and protected so thoroughly that an attacker with broad access still cannot reach them, which is why offline or otherwise segregated copies matter so much. And the slow, multi-stage progression means there is a window (often days or weeks) in which detection and response can stop the attack before the encryption ever fires, if the monitoring and operations capabilities of the later chapters are watching for the lateral movement and reconnaissance that precede it. Ransomware is, in this light, not a single catastrophic event to be survived but a process to be interrupted, and the organizations that fare best are those that detect the intrusion in its early stages rather than discovering it when the ransom note appears.

A working taxonomy of malware

The payloads attackers deliver are collectively called malware, and a working vocabulary helps you reason about defenses and prepares the ground for the malware-analysis chapter. A virus attaches itself to a legitimate file or program and spreads when that host is run or shared. A worm spreads on its own across networks without needing a host file or user action, which is what makes worms capable of explosive, self-propagating outbreaks. A trojan disguises itself as something benign to trick a user into running it, taking its name from the famous wooden horse. A rootkit hides deep in a system to conceal an attacker's presence and maintain stealthy access, often subverting the operating system itself so that ordinary tools cannot see it. Spyware quietly collects information, and a keylogger specifically records keystrokes to steal credentials. Ransomware, the dominant criminal threat of recent years, encrypts a victim's data and demands payment for the key, increasingly combined with extortion in which the attacker also steals the data and threatens to publish it, so that even a good backup does not fully neutralize the threat. Botnets are networks of compromised machines marshalled under central control for spam, denial-of-service, or further attacks. Fileless malware lives in memory and abuses legitimate system tools rather than dropping a recognizable malicious file, specifically to evade defenses that look for known bad files. Underlying many of these is the concept of an *exploit*, which is code that takes advantage of a specific vulnerability. A *zero-day* is an exploit for a flaw the defender does not yet know about yet and for which no patch exists, which is the rare and expensive capability that even good patching cannot stop and that therefore makes detection and containment indispensable.

Defense in depth: one wall is never enough

The central architectural idea that ties modern security together is defense in depth: the deliberate layering of multiple, independent controls so that no single failure leads to compromise. The metaphor is a castle—a moat, then walls, then guards, then a locked keep—where breaching one barrier only brings the attacker up against the next.

In modern systems, an attacker who slips past the perimeter firewall encounters endpoint protection. One who compromises a workstation meets network segmentation that limits lateral movement. One who reaches a database still faces encryption that renders stolen data useless without the keys. At every stage, logging and monitoring give defenders an opportunity to detect the attack and respond.

This approach works because controls fail. Every control has weaknesses, becomes misconfigured, or eventually encounters an attack it was never designed to stop. If security depends on any single mechanism being perfect, the organization will eventually be breached. Layering changes the problem: each control only has to be effective enough to slow, constrain, or expose the attacker because the remaining layers compensate for what it misses.

When evaluating a security control, the important question is therefore not only "does this help?" but also "what happens when it fails?" What is the next layer, and will defenders notice the failure in time to respond?

Several recurring principles make defense in depth practical in real systems:

- **Least privilege** gives every user, account, and process only the access required to perform its task and no more. When an account is compromised, the resulting damage is therefore limited. The over-privileged account is the attacker's dream because it turns one compromise into total access.

- **Hardening** means configuring systems to be defensible by default. Unnecessary software and services are removed, unused ports are closed, default passwords are changed, and obsolete protocols are disabled. The fewer exposed components a system has, the smaller its attack surface becomes.
- **Secure defaults** ensure that the safe choice is the automatic one. Systems that ship insecure and rely on administrators to manually lock them down frequently remain insecure in practice.
- **Separation of duties** ensures that no single individual can independently complete a sensitive action. The employee who requests a payment, for example, should not also approve it. This principle protects against both malicious insiders and catastrophic mistakes.
- **Fail securely** means systems fall back to a safe state when something breaks. A failed authentication service, for instance, should deny access rather than silently grant it.

These principles require more discipline than money, yet they prevent more real-world harm than many expensive security products. They recur throughout modern security architecture because they shape how secure systems behave even when individual controls inevitably fail.

Chapter 4: Encryption from the Ground Up and the Quantum Horizon

IN THIS CHAPTER

Why encryption deserves a chapter of its own

Encryption is the mathematical backbone of nearly every other control in this book. It is what makes a stolen drive useless, what protects a password as it crosses a café's Wi-Fi, what lets two strangers' computers establish a private channel across a hostile internet, what underpins the certificates that tell your browser a website is who it claims to be, and—as a later chapter explores at length—what now wraps the overwhelming majority of network traffic, with profound consequences for how you inspect and defend it. Yet encryption is widely treated as a black box, "we use encryption" said with the same finality as "we lock the doors," when in fact the details determine whether the lock is sound or theatrical. This chapter opens the box and walks through how encryption works at every level, then turns to the one development that could undermine much of it: quantum computing.

Symmetric encryption: one shared secret

The oldest and conceptually simplest form of cryptography is *symmetric encryption*, in which the same secret key is used both to encrypt and to decrypt data. The modern workhorse of symmetric cryptography is the *AES*, usually deployed with 128- or 256-bit keys and implemented so efficiently that many modern processors contain dedicated hardware instructions for it. Another widely used cipher is *ChaCha20*, which is especially valuable on systems without specialized AES hardware support. Because symmetric encryption is fast and computationally efficient, it performs the actual bulk encryption in most secure systems: files stored on disks, data traveling across networks, and the contents of encrypted web sessions are all typically protected with symmetric ciphers.

Its fundamental difficulty is key distribution and management. Because the same key both locks and unlocks the information, the communicating parties must somehow share that secret in advance without revealing it to an eavesdropper. If an attacker obtains the key, the security of the entire system collapses. Even more challenging is the problem of scale: in a network with many users, every pair of participants ideally requires its own secret key. If ten people all need to communicate privately with one another, dozens of separate keys must be created and securely distributed; in systems with thousands or millions of users, the number of required keys becomes enormous. Each key must not only be generated securely, but also exchanged, stored, rotated, revoked if compromised, and eventually replaced. Securely managing secret keys across an untrusted network is precisely the problem symmetric cryptography cannot solve by itself, and for much of the history of cryptography this was the central challenge of the field.

An important practical detail is that a symmetric cipher alone is not enough to define a secure encryption system. Many symmetric algorithms, including AES, operate on fixed-size blocks of data, and a separate procedure called a *mode of operation* determines how those blocks are encrypted across an entire message. The choice of mode is as important as the choice of cipher itself.

A poorly designed mode can leak information even when the underlying cipher is mathematically secure. For example, if identical plaintext blocks are always transformed into identical ciphertext blocks, repeated patterns in the original data remain visible after encryption. The classic demonstration is an encrypted bitmap image whose broad outlines are still recognizable because large regions of identical color produce repeating ciphertext patterns. Secure modes prevent this by ensuring that each block is encrypted in a way that depends on additional randomness or contextual information, so that even identical plaintext blocks produce completely different ciphertext.

Modern cryptography also requires protection against tampering, not merely secrecy. For this reason, contemporary systems generally use *authenticated encryption modes*, which provide integrity as well as confidentiality. In these schemes, any alteration of the ciphertext causes decryption to fail with an authentication error instead of producing corrupted plaintext. Names such as AES-GCM or ChaCha20-Poly1305 therefore describe not only the underlying cipher but also the mode in which it is used, and the use of an authenticated encryption mode is generally a sign of a modern and secure configuration.

Asymmetric encryption: a public and a private key

The breakthrough that solved the key-distribution problem was *asymmetric cryptography*, also called *public-key cryptography*. Instead of relying on a single shared secret, each participant possesses two mathematically related keys: a *public key*, which may be distributed openly to anyone, and a *private key*, which must remain secret. The relationship between the two keys is designed so that data encrypted with one key can only be decrypted with the other.

This arrangement fundamentally changes how secure communication can occur. In a symmetric system, two strangers cannot communicate securely until they somehow exchange a secret key in advance. Public-key cryptography removes that requirement. Anyone can obtain another person's public key and use it to encrypt a message, but only the holder of the corresponding private key can decrypt and read it. The public key may therefore be shared openly without weakening security, while the private key becomes the sole secret that must be protected.

The importance of this idea is difficult to overstate. Before public-key cryptography, secure communication at large scale was extraordinarily cumbersome because every pair of communicating parties needed a separate shared secret. A network of a million users would require an immense number of carefully distributed keys. Public-key systems make global secure communication practical because each user needs to manage only one long-term private key and publish only one corresponding public key.

The most historically important public-key algorithm is *RSA*, whose security depends on the practical difficulty of factoring extremely large integers. Although multiplying two large prime numbers together is computationally easy, reversing the process and determining the original primes from their product is believed to be prohibitively difficult for classical computers when sufficiently large numbers are used. This asymmetry between easy computation and difficult reversal forms the basis of RSA security. Modern systems increasingly favor *elliptic-curve cryptography* (ECC), which relies on mathematical properties of elliptic curves over finite fields. ECC provides comparable security with far smaller key sizes than RSA, reducing memory usage, bandwidth, and computational cost. This efficiency is especially valuable on mobile phones, embedded devices, and large internet services handling millions of encrypted connections simultaneously. Algorithms such as Curve25519 and P-256 are widely deployed examples of elliptic-curve systems.

A closely related concept is the *Diffie–Hellman key exchange*, one of the most important inventions in the history of cryptography. Diffie–Hellman does not directly encrypt messages. Instead, it allows two parties who have never met to establish a shared secret over a public channel without ever transmitting that secret itself. Even an eavesdropper who records the entire exchange cannot feasibly reconstruct the resulting key. This capability forms the conceptual foundation of modern secure communication protocols because it allows strangers on the internet to create encryption keys dynamically and securely.

Despite its revolutionary advantages, asymmetric cryptography has important limitations. Public-key operations are computationally expensive compared with symmetric encryption, often slower by orders of magnitude. Encrypting large files or high-volume network traffic directly with RSA or elliptic-curve operations would be inefficient and impractical. Asymmetric cryptography is therefore used sparingly, primarily for authentication, digital signatures, and secure key exchange rather than for bulk data encryption itself.

The hybrid approach: how they work together

Modern secure systems therefore combine symmetric and asymmetric cryptography into a hybrid design that exploits the strengths of each. Symmetric encryption is extremely fast but cannot distribute keys securely on its own. Asymmetric cryptography solves the key-distribution problem but is computationally expensive. Used together, they create systems that are both practical and secure.

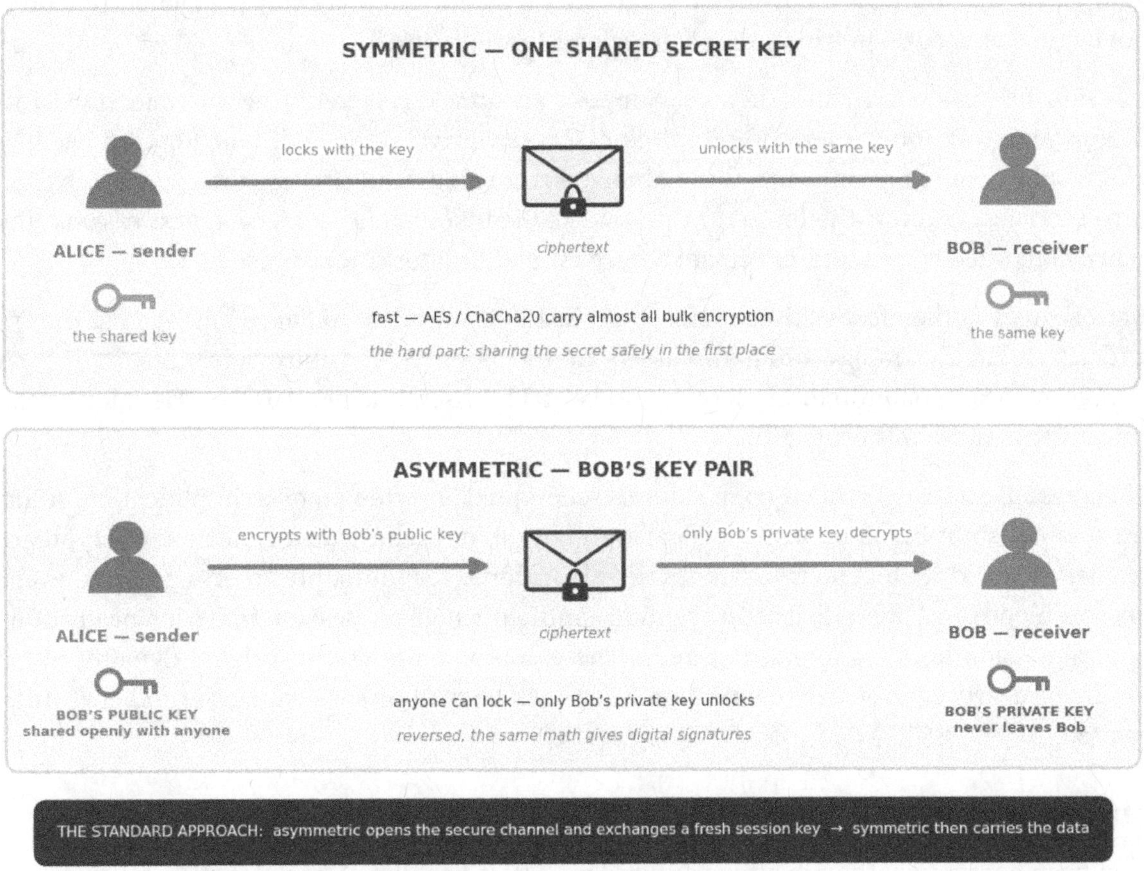

FIGURE 4.1 Symmetric and asymmetric encryption — each solves the other's hard part, which is why real systems are hybrids.

This hybrid architecture underlies essentially all secure internet communication, including Transport Layer Security, the protocol responsible for securing web traffic, online banking, messaging applications, and countless other digital services.

A secure connection typically begins with a handshake. During this phase, the communicating parties use asymmetric cryptography to authenticate identities and establish a shared secret securely across the public network. This process often involves digital certificates, public keys, and ephemeral Diffie–Hellman exchanges. Once both sides derive the same fresh symmetric key—called a *session key*—the asymmetric operations largely stop and is discarded after use.

From that point onward, the actual conversation is encrypted using fast symmetric algorithms such as AES or ChaCha20. The asymmetric component solves the problem of trust and key exchange; the symmetric component performs the computationally intensive task of encrypting the data stream efficiently. In effect, public-key cryptography opens the secure channel, while symmetric cryptography carries the conversation.

An important modern security property is *forward secrecy* (sometimes called *perfect forward secrecy*). In systems with forward secrecy, the session keys used to encrypt individual conversations are temporary and derived independently for each session. They are not permanently stored and cannot be reconstructed later from the server's long-term private key alone.

This design has profound consequences. Suppose an attacker secretly records encrypted internet traffic for years and only later compromises a server's private key. Without forward secrecy, the attacker could potentially return to those archived recordings and decrypt them retroactively. With forward secrecy, however, the long-term private key is insufficient to recover past session keys, so previously recorded conversations remain secure even after later compromise.

Forward secrecy is therefore a direct defense against long-term surveillance and against the "record now, decrypt later" strategy often discussed in the context of future advances in computing, including quantum computing. Modern versions of TLS use ephemeral Diffie–Hellman exchanges specifically to achieve this protection.

For this reason, asking whether a connection is "encrypted" is often an oversimplification. A modern secure session is not based on a single algorithm but on an orchestrated collection of cryptographic mechanisms working together: asymmetric algorithms for authentication and key exchange, symmetric algorithms for efficient encryption, authenticated modes for integrity protection, and ephemeral session keys for forward secrecy. These components are negotiated dynamically at the beginning of nearly every secure connection, with each algorithm performing the role for which it is best suited.

Hashing: one-way fingerprints

Distinct from encryption, though often confused with it, is hashing. A hash function takes data of any size and produces a fixed-length fingerprint. Crucially, hashing is one-way: the fingerprint cannot be reversed to recover the original data. The same input will always produce the same fingerprint, but even a one-character change in the input will produce a completely different result, in a way that is not predictable. Hashing is therefore a tool for verifying integrity. When data is passed through a specific hashing algorithm, the algorithm produces a fingerprint based on the contents of that data. To check whether a message has been altered, a system can compare the hash calculated before transmission with the hash calculated after the message is received and decrypted. If the fingerprints match, the data has not changed. If they differ, the data has been modified.

Modern algorithms like the SHA-2 family are used for general integrity, while password storage uses deliberately slow, salted functions like bcrypt or Argon2, where the *salt* is a random value mixed into each password so that identical passwords produce different hashes and precomputed attack tables become useless, and the slowness deliberately frustrates the brute-force guessing that a fast hash would permit. The key mental distinction to carry forward: encryption is reversible by design with the right key, while hashing is irreversible by design, and using one where you need the other is a common and serious error.

One final point is that hashing is also commonly used to protect the confidentiality of stored passwords. Instead of storing the password itself, a system stores a hash of the password. When a user tries to log in, the system hashes the password attempt and compares that result with the stored hash in its database. If the two hashes match, the system can verify the password without needing to store or reveal the original password. However, the one nuance is that hashing only protects the password at rest, not when a user types or sends their password to be checked against a system's database. There are ways to exploit the use of password hashes to authenticate into a system, but that is beyond the scope of this book.

Digital signatures and the chain of trust

Combining cryptographic hashing with asymmetric keys produces *digital signatures*, one of the foundational mechanisms of modern computer security. Digital signatures simultaneously provide integrity, authenticity, and non-repudiation. To create a signature, the signer first computes a cryptographic hash of the data and then uses their private key to sign that hash. Anyone possessing the corresponding public key can verify the signature by checking that it matches the hash of the received data. If the values agree, the recipient gains two assurances at once: the data has not been altered, and it was signed by whoever controls the private key. Because the private key is presumed to be under the sole control of its owner, the signer also cannot plausibly deny having created the signature later. Digital signatures therefore serve as the cryptographic equivalent of sealed and witnessed documents, though with far stronger mathematical guarantees.

This mechanism underlies a remarkable amount of modern computing. Software vendors sign operating-system updates so users can verify that the updates genuinely originated from the vendor and were not modified in transit. Developers sign applications so operating systems can warn users when software comes from an unknown or untrusted source. Electronic document-signing systems rely on digital signatures to authenticate contracts and records. Most importantly for everyday internet use, digital signatures form the basis of the certificates that authenticate websites and make secure web browsing possible.

Yet digital signatures alone do not solve the entire trust problem. A signature can prove that a message came from the holder of a certain private key, but it does not automatically prove whose key that is. If an attacker could trick you into accepting their public key while claiming it belonged to your bank, then they could sign fraudulent messages that would appear valid. The critical question therefore becomes not merely "Is this signature mathematically correct?" but "Can I trust that this public key genuinely belongs to the claimed identity?"

The answer is a system known as *public key infrastructure* (PKI), a global framework designed to establish trust in public keys. At the center of PKI are organizations called *certificate authorities* (CAs). A certificate authority acts as a trusted third party that verifies identities and issues *digital certificates*: standardized electronic documents that bind a public key to a specific identity, such as a domain name, organization, or individual.

The standard format for these certificates is known as X.509. An X.509 certificate contains information such as:

- the identity of the certificate holder,
- the holder's public key,
- the name of the issuing certificate authority,

- the period during which the certificate is valid,
- and the digital signature of the authority itself.

Conceptually, a certificate is similar to a passport or notarized credential. The certificate authority is asserting: "We have verified that this public key belongs to this entity." The authority then digitally signs the certificate with its own private key so that anyone can verify the claim using the authority's public key.

This immediately raises another question: why trust the certificate authority? Public key infrastructure solves this recursively through a chain of trust. Modern operating systems and web browsers ship with a small built-in collection of highly trusted root certificates, belonging to major certificate authorities. These roots function as the anchors of trust for the entire system.

Root certificate authorities rarely issue website certificates directly. Instead, they usually sign certificates for intermediate authorities, which are delegated the power to issue certificates to end entities such as websites. This layered structure improves operational security because the highly sensitive root keys can remain offline and rarely used, while intermediates handle day-to-day certificate issuance.

When a user visits a secure website, the site presents its certificate along with any necessary intermediate certificates. The browser then performs a sequence of checks:

- It verifies that each certificate in the chain is digitally signed by the next authority above it.
- It follows the chain upward until it reaches a trusted root certificate already stored in the operating system or browser.
- It confirms that the certificate has not expired and is currently within its valid time period.
- It verifies that the certificate was issued for the domain name the user is actually visiting.
- It checks whether the certificate permits the intended usage, such as server authentication.
- It determines whether the certificate has been revoked because of compromise, misuse, or administrative invalidation.

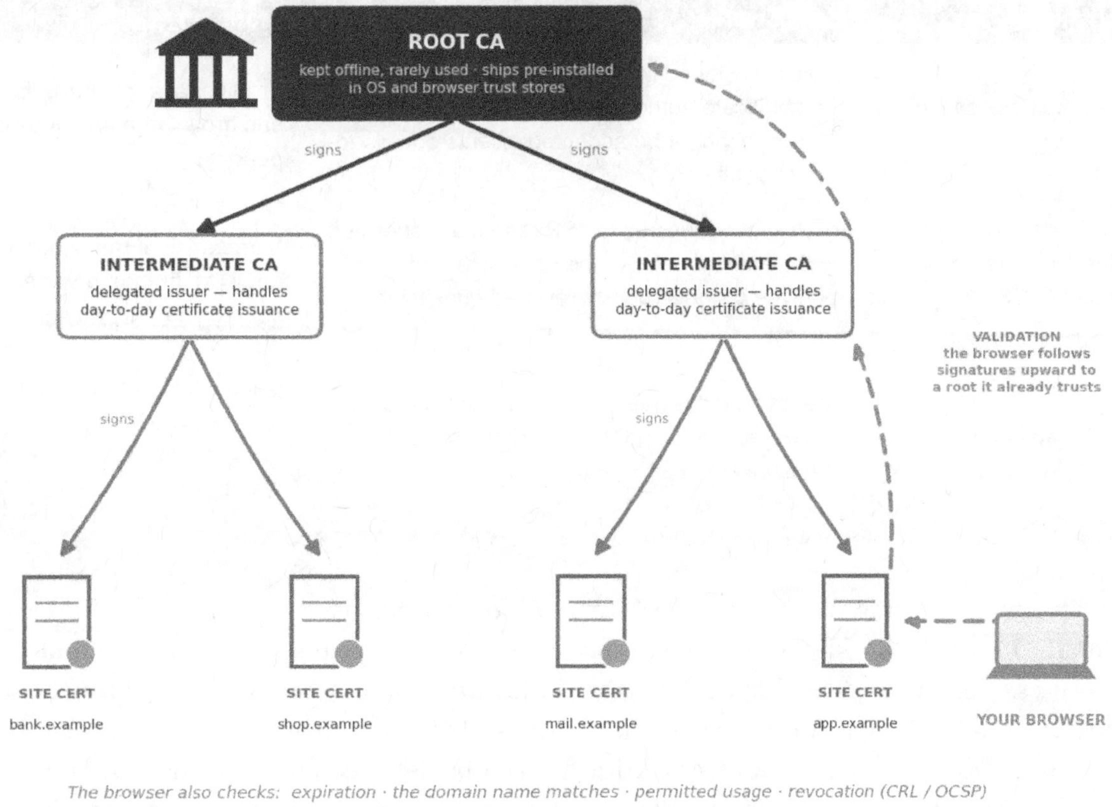

FIGURE 4.2 The chain of trust — from an offline root, through intermediates, to the certificates websites present.

Revocation is an important but often overlooked part of PKI. Certificates are issued with expiration dates, but problems can arise long before a certificate naturally expires. A private key may be stolen, a certificate authority may discover that it issued a certificate fraudulently or incorrectly, or an organization may simply wish to discontinue use of a certificate. In these cases, the certificate authority must be able to mark the certificate as no longer trustworthy.

One traditional mechanism for this is the *Certificate Revocation List* (CRL). A CRL is a digitally signed list published periodically by the certificate authority containing the serial numbers of certificates that should no longer be accepted. Browsers and operating systems can download these lists and check whether a presented certificate appears on them.

A more modern and efficient mechanism is the *Online Certificate Status Protocol* (OCSP). Instead of downloading a potentially large revocation list, the client sends a direct query to an OCSP responder operated by the certificate authority asking whether a particular certificate is still valid. The responder returns a signed answer indicating whether the certificate is good, revoked, or unknown. Many systems also support *OCSP stapling*, in which the website itself periodically fetches a signed OCSP response from the authority and "staples" it to the TLS handshake, reducing latency and improving privacy because the browser no longer needs to contact the authority directly.

TABLE 4.1 Certificate revocation mechanisms

Mechanism	How it works	Trade-off
Certificate Revocation List (CRL)	A digitally signed list, published periodically by the certificate authority, of serial numbers that should no longer be accepted; clients download and check it	Traditional and simple, but lists can grow large and updates are periodic
Online Certificate Status Protocol (OCSP)	The client queries an OCSP responder operated by the authority about one certificate and receives a signed good / revoked / unknown answer	More efficient than downloading a full list, but the browser must contact the authority
OCSP stapling	The website itself periodically fetches a signed OCSP response and "staples" it to the TLS handshake	Reduces latency and improves privacy. The browser no longer needs to contact the authority directly.

Browsers and operating systems may perform additional protective checks as well. Modern browsers maintain internal blocklists of known malicious or compromised certificates and certificate authorities. Some browsers implement *certificate pinning* or maintain logs through *Certificate Transparency*, a public auditing system in which newly issued certificates are recorded in append-only public ledgers so that fraudulent certificates can be detected and investigated. Major browsers can also remove trust from entire certificate authorities if they repeatedly violate security standards or are compromised.

Only if all of these checks succeed does the browser treat the connection as authenticated and establish a secure encrypted session. The familiar padlock icon in a web browser therefore represents not just encryption, but the successful validation of an entire hierarchy of cryptograpic trust.

This infrastructure is one of the quiet foundations of the modern internet. It allows strangers across the world to establish authenticated encrypted connections instantly, without ever having met or exchanged keys beforehand. Every secure web session, software update, app installation, and cloud login depends on this system functioning correctly.

At the same time, public key infrastructure creates concentrated points of trust and power. Because browsers inherently trust root certificate authorities, any authority capable of issuing certificates can, in principle, issue a certificate for any domain. If a certificate authority is compromised, coerced, or acts maliciously, attackers may be able to impersonate legitimate websites convincingly enough to intercept encrypted traffic. For this reason, certificate authorities are among the most security-sensitive organizations on the internet.

The same mechanism is also deliberately replicated inside many organizations. Companies, universities, and governments often install their own internal root certificate authorities onto managed devices. Once those devices trust the organization's internal authority, the organization can generate certificates for external websites on demand and transparently intercept encrypted traffic passing through its networks. Technically, this works because the device now trusts the organization's root certificate just as it trusts commercial internet authorities. As later discussions of encrypted-traffic inspection will show, the very infrastructure that makes secure communication with strangers possible at internet scale is also what enables institutions to inspect, filter, and monitor encrypted communications within their own environments.

The three states of data, and where decryption must happen

Encryption protects data in three states, and a complete posture addresses all three. *Data in transit*—moving across networks—is protected by transport encryption like TLS, realized in practice through the secure web connections, the VPNs, and the encrypted application protocols of later chapters. *Data at rest*—sitting in storage—is protected by disk, database, or file encryption, the backstop that makes a stolen drive worthless and turns a lost laptop from a breach into an inconvenience. The third and trickiest state is *data in use*—being actively processed—because, with narrow exceptions, data must be decrypted into memory to be operated on; a processor cannot, in the general case, add two encrypted numbers or run a query against an encrypted database without first decrypting. This is why a careful data-handling clause specifies that data may be decrypted only transiently, in volatile memory, solely to the extent necessary to do the work, and must be re-encrypted before it is written anywhere or transmitted onward. Emerging techniques push at this limit. ***Confidential computing* uses hardware-isolated enclaves to protect data even while in use, and *homomorphic encryption* allows certain computations directly on encrypted data without ever decrypting it, but these remain specialized and costly, so for almost all systems the practical reality is encryption in transit and at rest combined with disciplined, transient decryption during processing.**

The TLS handshake, step by step

Transport Layer Security, almost always abbreviated TLS, is the cryptographic protocol that secures data in transit across networks, and it is the most widely used security protocol on the internet. A *protocol*, in this sense, is simply an agreed set of rules two parties follow in order to communicate; TLS is the set of rules by which two computers establish an encrypted, authenticated channel and then exchange data through it safely. It is what puts the S in HTTPS: when a browser connects to a website securely, TLS is the machinery working beneath the padlock. TLS does not replace the ordinary transport that carries internet traffic; it wraps it, sitting just above the transport layer so that the applications above (web browsing, email delivery, and countless others) gain confidentiality, integrity, and authentication without having to implement cryptography themselves. In a single connection it delivers all three of the protections this chapter has described: it encrypts the data so that eavesdroppers see only ciphertext, it integrity-protects it so that tampering is detected, and it authenticates the server and client through the certificates and public-key infrastructure described above, so that you can trust you are talking to the genuine site rather than an impostor.

TLS evolved from an older protocol called *Secure Sockets Layer*, or SSL, which is why people still loosely say "SSL" when they mean TLS and why the two are often written together as "SSL/TLS"; the SSL versions are long obsolete and insecure, and the name survives mostly by habit. TLS itself has gone through versions, and here currency matters as it does for any cryptography: the modern, recommended versions are TLS 1.2 and the faster, streamlined TLS 1.3, while earlier versions carry known weaknesses and should be disabled, exactly the "no weak protocols" discipline urged throughout this book. Beyond securing web traffic, TLS underpins a great deal more that appears in later chapters: the TLS-based VPNs of the network-defense chapter, the encrypted mail transport of the email chapter, and the secure connections that applications and APIs depend on.

The heart of TLS is the *handshake*—the brief negotiation that occurs before any real data flows—and tracing it concretely is the clearest way to watch the abstract pieces of this chapter assemble into a working secure channel. When your browser connects securely to a website, that handshake plays out in a few quick steps. First, the client announces itself, offering the versions and cryptographic options it supports: a negotiation, because both sides must agree on algorithms they share. The server responds by selecting from those options and, decisively, presenting its certificate: the signed statement, traceable through the chain of trust to a root the client already trusts, that binds the server's public key to its identity. The client validates this certificate (checking the signature chain, the expiration, the revocation status, and that the name matches the site it intended to reach) and if any check fails, a well-behaved client refuses to proceed, which is exactly the protection a user relies on and exactly what the decryption chapter must carefully preserve when it interposes a firewall.

With the server authenticated, the two sides perform the key exchange that is the heart of the matter. Using asymmetric techniques, most often an ephemeral Diffie-Hellman exchange, provides the forward secrecy described above, and they derive a shared symmetric session key over the public connection without ever transmitting the key itself, so that even an eavesdropper recording every byte cannot reconstruct it. From that point the handshake completes, both sides confirm they have arrived at the same key, and the connection switches to fast symmetric encryption with authenticated modes for the actual data. The whole exchange takes a fraction of a second, happens before the user sees anything, and recurs for essentially every secure connection a device makes, billions of times over. Understanding it clarifies several things this book relies on: why the certificate and its validation are so central, why a compromised certificate authority is catastrophic, why forward secrecy defeats the patient "record now, decrypt later" attacker, and why a firewall that wishes to inspect this traffic must insert itself into precisely this exchange with a certificate the client will accept. The handshake is where confidentiality, authenticity, and integrity are negotiated into existence on every secure link, and it is the same dance whether the link protects a banking session, a VPN tunnel, or a malware download.

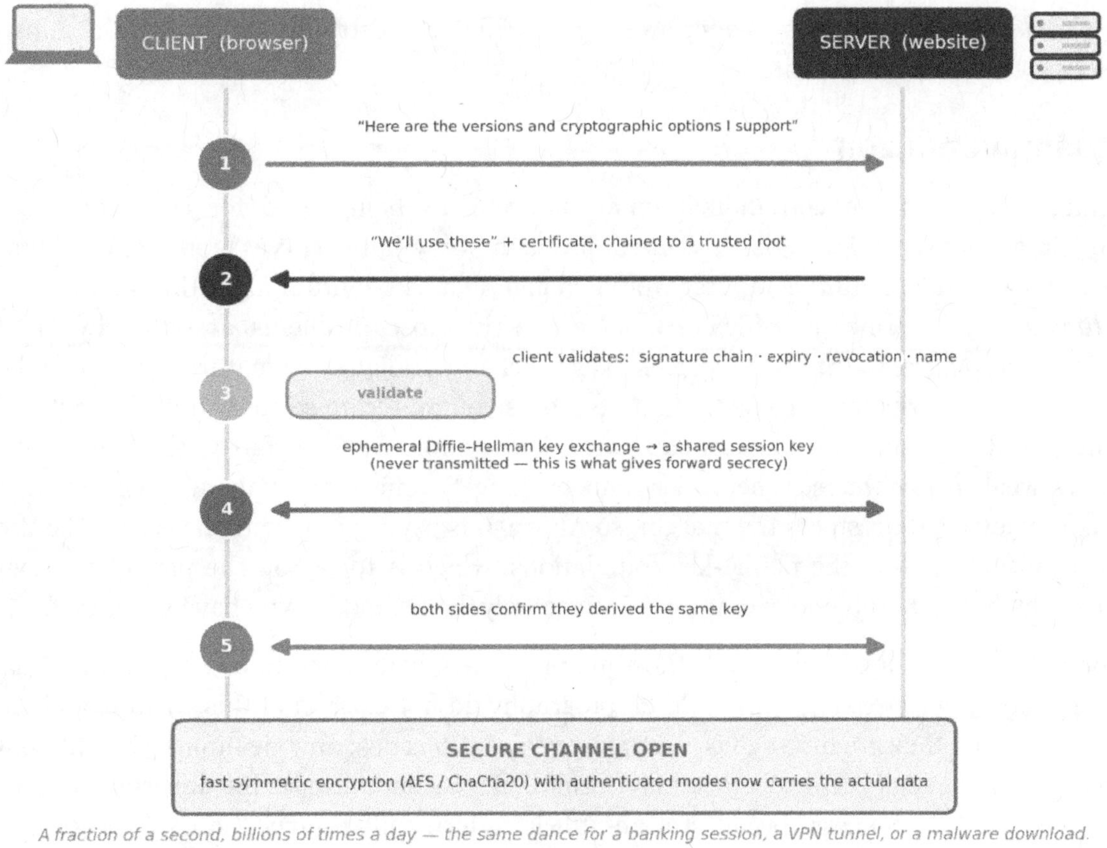

FIGURE 4.3 The TLS handshake — negotiate, authenticate, exchange keys, confirm; then fast symmetric encryption carries the data.

Key management: where encryption actually lives or dies

Encryption is only ever as strong as the management of its keys. The strongest algorithm in the world protects nothing if the key is left in a configuration file, shared by email, hard-coded into source code, never rotated, or impossible to revoke when an employee leaves. Good key management spans the whole lifecycle: generating keys with genuine randomness, because predictable keys are no keys at all; storing them in protected hardware rather than alongside the data they protect; controlling who and what may use them, with least privilege applied as rigorously as to any account; rotating them periodically so that a compromise has a limited window of value; and destroying them securely at end of life. The protected hardware in question is the *cryptographic module* discussed in the compliance chapter: the bounded, ideally validated component that holds keys and performs operations without letting the raw key material escape. In cloud environments this typically takes the form of a *key management service* backed by *hardware security modules*: the provider operates the modules, but the customer controls the key policy: who can use a key, when to disable or delete it, how often it rotates. A consequence worth understanding is that in such arrangements the customer often cannot physically extract the raw key bytes, because the module is designed never to release them; this is a feature, not a flaw, and it is why a sound contractual termination requirement asks that keys be disabled and destroyed rather than "returned." Destroying the key renders the data it protected permanently unrecoverable even if copies of the ciphertext remain: a technique called *crypto-shredding* that is often a cleaner and more verifiable end-of-life remedy than chasing down and deleting every copy of the data.

The quantum horizon

Everything above rests on certain mathematical problems being hard for computers to solve: factoring large numbers for RSA, a related problem for elliptic curves and Diffie-Hellman. A sufficiently powerful quantum computer would change that. A quantum algorithm known as *Shor's algorithm* could, in principle, efficiently solve exactly those problems and thereby break the asymmetric cryptography that underpins key exchange, digital signatures, and public key infrastructure: the very mechanisms that let strangers communicate securely and that authenticate everything from websites to software updates. The symmetric side fares far better: quantum computing weakens symmetric encryption and hashing by effectively halving their strength, but doubling the key length restores the margin, so AES-256 is expected to remain secure. The threat is therefore concentrated on the public-key foundations, which is to say on the part of cryptography that solves the hardest problem: communicating securely with someone you have never met.

Two honest caveats temper this. First, the timeline is genuinely uncertain: large, stable quantum computers capable of breaking real-world cryptography do not exist as of this writing, and credible estimates for when they might range across many years to decades; anyone offering a confident date is guessing, and the engineering obstacles are formidable. Second, despite the uncertainty, the threat is not purely a future concern, because of an attack pattern called *harvest now, decrypt later*: an adversary can record encrypted data today and simply wait, decrypting it once quantum capability arrives. For data that must stay confidential for many years (state secrets, long-lived intellectual property, certain medical and financial records, etc.) the relevant question is not "is quantum here yet?" but "will this data still matter when it arrives?", and for some data the prudent answer is to act now.

The response is *post-quantum cryptography*: new algorithms based on mathematical problems believed hard even for quantum computers. Standards bodies have moved this from theory toward practice, with the first post-quantum algorithms for key establishment and digital signatures now standardized and beginning to appear in mainstream software and protocols. For practitioners today, the prudent posture is not panic but preparation, and the single most useful concept is *crypto-agility*: designing and procuring systems so that the cryptographic algorithms can be swapped out without rebuilding everything around them. Organizations that hardwired specific algorithms deep into their systems will face a painful migration; those that built in agility will adapt as the standards mature and the threat clarifies. When you evaluate products and architectures now, asking how readily their cryptography can be upgraded is no longer premature: it is foresight, and given the uncertainty it is the one move that pays off under every plausible timeline, because a system that can change its algorithms cheaply is protected whether quantum-arrives soon, late, or never. Because standards and timelines in this area are evolving, treat the specifics here as a snapshot and verify the current state of post-quantum standardization when it bears on a real decision.

Chapter 5: Identity and Access Management

IN THIS CHAPTER

Identity is the new perimeter
Authentication and the factors of proof
Single sign-on and federation
Federation: trust between different systems
The three common protocols
Authorization: deciding what is allowed
The identity lifecycle and the danger of orphaned accounts
Privileged access: guarding the keys to the kingdom

Identity is the new perimeter

For most of security's history, the model was a hard outer wall with a trusted interior: the firewall kept the bad people out, and everyone inside was assumed friendly. That model has eroded almost to nothing. With cloud services, remote work, mobile devices, and third-party integrations, there is no longer a clean inside and outside; your data lives in a dozen places you do not own, accessed by people on networks you do not control. What remains constant across all of it is who is asking for access. This is why identity has become the real perimeter, and why identity and access management, the discipline of knowing who someone is and controlling what they can do, has moved from a back-office concern to the center of security. It is no accident that the firewall chapters ahead treat the user's identity as a first-class input to policy, or that the zero-trust architecture later in the book is built on identity above all; the entire modern edifice rests on getting identity right.

It helps to separate three ideas that are often run together. *Authentication* is establishing who you are. *Authorization* is determining what you are allowed to do once your identity is established. *Accounting*, or *audit*, is recording what you actually did. A great many security failures trace to confusion among these: granting authorization without solid authentication, or having neither audit nor the ability to reconstruct who did what after an incident. The three together are sometimes called the *triple-A of access*, and a mature system addresses all three deliberately rather than assuming that authenticating someone is the end of the matter.

Authentication and the factors of proof

Authentication rests on factors, traditionally grouped as *something you know* (a password or PIN), *something you have* (a phone, a hardware token, a smart card), and *something you are* (a fingerprint, a face, or another biometric). A password alone, a single knowledge factor, is the weakest common form, because passwords are guessed, reused across sites, phished, and stolen in enormous breaches, and a stolen password is indistinguishable from the real user. The decisive improvement is *multi-factor authentication*, which requires two or more factors of different types, so that a stolen password alone is not enough; an attacker would also need the user's physical device or biometric. Multi-factor authentication is, dollar for dollar, the single most effective control most organizations can deploy, because it defeats the vast category of attacks that depend on stolen or guessed credentials, and that category is enormous, encompassing most of the initial-access techniques attackers actually use. If you make one improvement after reading this book, make it universal multi-factor authentication on everything that supports it, starting with email, remote access, and administrative accounts.

Not all second factors are equal, and the differences matter. A code sent by text message is far better than nothing but can be intercepted, redirected by tricking a mobile carrier, or phished by a convincing fake login page that relays the code in real time. An authenticator app that generates time-based codes is stronger, since there is no carrier to subvert, but it can still be phished by relay. The strongest widely available option is a hardware security key or passkey built on the FIDO2 standard, which is phishing-resistant by design because it cryptographically binds the login to the legitimate website's address and simply will not produce a valid response to an impostor site, no matter how convincing that site looks to the human. The industry is moving toward *passwordless authentication* built on these methods, especially passkeys that replace passwords entirely with a private key held on your device and unlocked by a biometric or PIN, precisely because it removes the password, the most attacked element, from the equation altogether. Where you can deploy phishing-resistant authentication for high-value accounts, you should, because it closes the door that most sophisticated credential attacks try to walk through.

Single sign-on and federation

As organizations increasingly rely on large numbers of cloud services, internal applications, and external platforms, requiring users to maintain separate usernames and passwords for every system becomes impractical and insecure. Users often respond by reusing passwords, choosing weak passwords, or storing credentials insecurely. At the same time, organizations must manage authentication data across many systems, increasing administrative complexity and security risk.

To address these problems, many organizations implement *single sign-on (SSO)*. Single sign-on allows a user to authenticate once with a centralized identity system and then access multiple applications without signing in again for each one. The centralized system responsible for authenticating users is called an *identity provider (IdP)*. The applications that rely on the identity provider for authentication are known as *service providers (SPs)* or *relying parties*.

For example, an employee may log in once to the organization's identity provider using a password and multifactor authentication. After successful authentication, the employee can open email, file-sharing services, human resources systems, and collaboration platforms without entering credentials again. The connected applications trust the identity provider's confirmation of the user's identity.

Single sign-on provides both operational and security advantages. Centralized authentication allows organizations to enforce consistent password policies and multifactor authentication requirements across all connected systems. User accounts can be disabled quickly from a single location when employees leave the organization, immediately revoking access to connected applications. In addition, reducing the number of systems that store passwords lowers the organization's overall exposure to credential theft.

SSO improves convenience, but it is also a major security improvement when implemented properly:

- There is one central place to enforce strong passwords and multifactor authentication.
- User accounts can be disabled immediately across all connected systems when an employee leaves.
- Fewer passwords are stored across different applications, reducing exposure if one application is compromised.
- Security teams can monitor authentication activity from a single central system.

Despite these advantages, SSO also concentrates risk. If attackers compromise the central identity provider, they may gain access to every connected application. For this reason, identity systems are considered highly critical infrastructure and must be protected with strong authentication, careful monitoring, logging, and strict administrative controls.

Federation: trust between different systems

Single sign-on often extends beyond a single organization through the use of *federation*. Federation is a trust relationship in which one system accepts authentication performed by another trusted system.

In a federated environment, the identity provider authenticates the user, and external applications trust the identity provider's assertion that the user has been successfully verified. This eliminates the need for every service to maintain separate user accounts and passwords.

IN PRACTICE — FEDERATION AT A UNIVERSITY

For example, a university may maintain a centralized identity provider for students and faculty. The university also subscribes to external services such as online research databases, cloud collaboration tools, and digital textbook platforms. When a student attempts to access one of these external services, the service redirects the student to the university's login system. After the student authenticates successfully, the university identity provider sends confirmation of the student's identity back to the external service. Because the service trusts the university's identity provider, access is granted without requiring a separate account or password for that service.

Rather than requiring students to create separate accounts for every vendor:

- The student visits the research database website.
- The database redirects the student to the university login page.
- The student signs in using university credentials.
- The university identity provider tells the database, "This person is an authenticated student."
- The database trusts the university and grants access.

The research database never needs to store the student's password. It simply trusts the university's identity system.

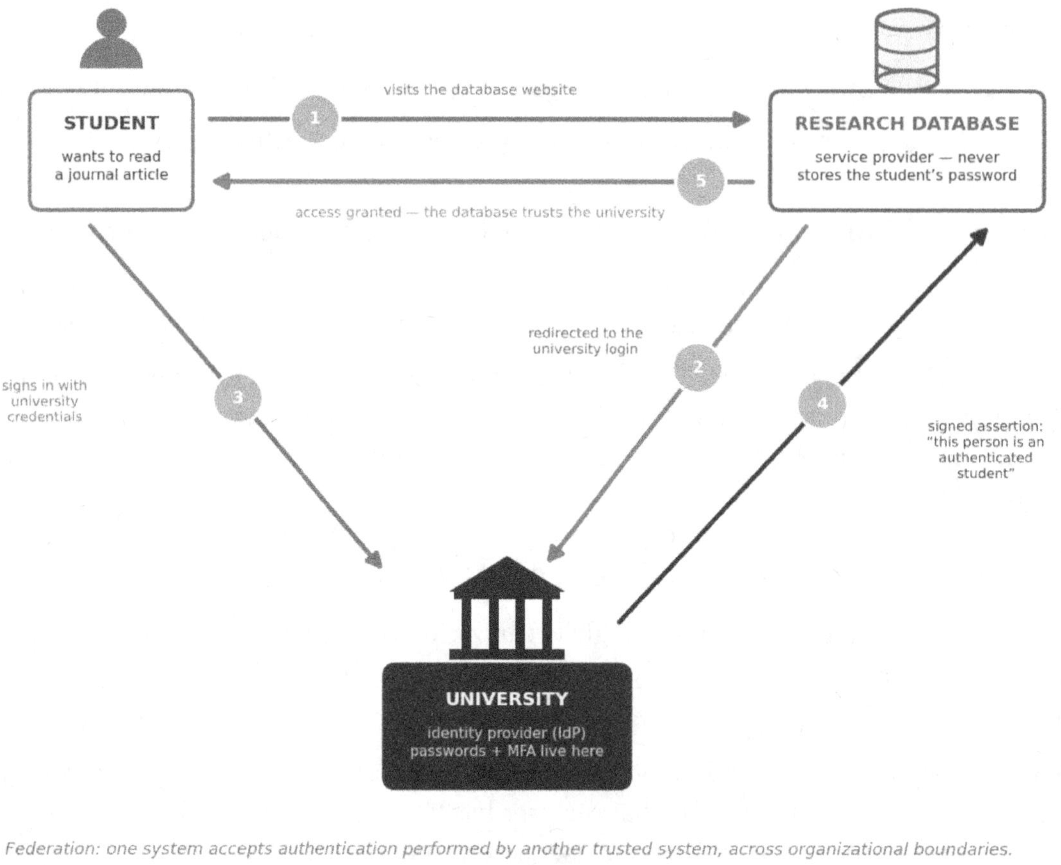

FIGURE 5.1 Federation — the research database trusts the university's identity provider; the password never leaves home.

Federation therefore enables authentication and access control across organizational boundaries while reducing password sprawl and administrative overhead.

The three common protocols

SAML

Security Assertion Markup Language (SAML) is a widely used standard for enterprise single sign-on. SAML is primarily designed for authentication, meaning it is used to verify a user's identity.

In a typical SAML authentication process, the user first attempts to access a web application. The application redirects the user to an identity provider. After the user authenticates successfully, the identity provider sends the application a digitally signed SAML assertion. This assertion contains information about the authenticated user, such as the user's identity and the time of authentication. Because the assertion is digitally signed, the application can verify that it originated from a trusted identity provider and was not altered during transmission.

A common example of SAML is enterprise access to internal business applications. An employee attempting to access a payroll or human resources portal may be redirected to the organization's authentication system. After successful login, the identity provider sends a signed SAML assertion to the application, allowing the employee to access the service without the application directly handling the employee's password.

SAML is especially common in large organizations and legacy enterprise environments. It is heavily associated with browser-based web applications and enterprise identity management systems.

The key purpose of SAML is summarized by the question "Who is the user?"

OAuth 2.0

OAuth 2.0 is an authorization framework rather than an authentication protocol. Its primary purpose is to allow one application to access resources stored in another application on behalf of a user, without requiring the user to share their password.

OAuth works by issuing access tokens that grant limited permissions to an application. Instead of giving an application full account credentials, the user authorizes a specific set of actions. For example, a calendar scheduling application may request permission to read a user's online calendar. The user authenticates directly with the calendar provider and then approves the requested permissions. The calendar provider issues the scheduling application an access token that allows only the approved actions, such as reading calendar events or creating meeting invitations. The scheduling application never learns the user's actual password.

OAuth is commonly used when third-party applications require controlled access to user data stored in another service. It supports delegated access while limiting unnecessary exposure of credentials.

The key purpose of OAuth is summarized by the question: "What is this application allowed to do?"

Because OAuth is designed for authorization rather than authentication, treating an OAuth access token as proof of identity can lead to serious security errors if used alone

OpenID Connect

OpenID Connect (OIDC) is an authentication protocol built on top of OAuth 2.0. It extends OAuth by adding identity information that allows applications to authenticate users.

While OAuth only provides authorization, OpenID Connect adds an ID token that contains verified information about the authenticated user. This token is commonly formatted as a JSON Web Token (JWT) and may include information such as the user's unique identifier, email address, and authentication time.

OpenID Connect is widely used in modern web and mobile applications and powers many common "Sign in with Google," "Sign in with Microsoft," and similar login systems. For example, when a user selects "Sign in with Google" on a website, the website redirects the user to Google's authentication system. After the user successfully authenticates and consents to share identity information, Google sends the website an ID token confirming the user's identity. The website then creates a session for the authenticated user without directly handling the user's password.

Because OpenID Connect builds on OAuth 2.0, it combines authentication and authorization capabilities. OAuth provides delegated access through access tokens, while OpenID Connect provides identity verification through ID tokens. The key purpose of OpenID Connect is summarized by the question: "Who is the user, using OAuth as the underlying framework?"

Three protocols dominate, and it is worth knowing what each is for, because they are constantly confused. The table below summarizes the protocols.

TABLE 5.1 The three common identity protocols

Protocol	What it is and what it is for
SAML	The established standard for enterprise web single sign-on, common in corporate applications, exchanging signed assertions about who a user is.
OAuth 2.0	An authorization framework for delegated access. It lets a user authorize one application to access specific resources in another application without giving that application their password (e.g. calendar, contacts, etc.).
OpenID Connect	A thin authentication layer built on top of OAuth; it powers the familiar "sign in with" buttons that let you log into one site using another's identity.

SAML and OpenID Connect prove who you are; OAuth grants permission to act on your behalf.

The short version to carry: SAML and OpenID Connect prove who you are; OAuth grants permission to act on your behalf, and conflating the two leads to real security mistakes, such as treating a permission grant as if it were proof of identity.

Authorization: deciding what is allowed

Once identity is established, authorization decides what that identity may do, and the governing principle is *least privilege* introduced earlier: grant exactly what is needed and no more, so that any compromised account can touch as little as possible. The common model for managing this at scale is *role-based access control*, where permissions attach to roles such as "accountant" or "support agent" and users are assigned roles, so that access is managed in coherent groups rather than one permission at a time, and a person's access changes cleanly when their role changes. A more flexible and granular approach, *attribute-based access control*, makes decisions from a richer set of attributes, including the user's department, the device's health, the time of day, the sensitivity of the resource, and the location of the request. This is the kind of contextual decision-making that zero trust and modern firewall policy both depend on. The two are not mutually exclusive; many environments use roles as the backbone and attributes to refine the edges.

The identity lifecycle and the danger of orphaned accounts

Identity is not a one-time grant but a lifecycle, often summarized as joiner, mover, leaver. When someone joins, they should be provisioned with exactly the access their role requires. It should be no more than needed, granted promptly so they can work, but scoped tightly. When they move, changing roles, teams, or responsibilities, their access should change with them, and here a quiet danger accumulates: *privilege creep*, in which people retain access from old roles that is never removed, gradually becoming over-privileged until a long-tenured employee holds the keys to half the organization for reasons no one remembers. When someone leaves, their access must be promptly and completely revoked. The leaver case is where organizations fail most visibly and most dangerously, because an *orphaned account* is an account that is still active after its owner has departed. It is a back door with no one watching it, and departed employees with lingering access are a recurring theme in real breaches, whether the former employee abuses it themselves or an attacker finds the forgotten account. Automating provisioning and especially deprovisioning, so that access reliably follows the person's actual employment status pulled from an authoritative source, closes a gap that manual processes leave open with depressing regularity. The same discipline applies to *non-human identities*, including service accounts, API keys, and machine credentials, which proliferate quietly, often outnumber human accounts, and are even more likely to be forgotten because no one ever leaves the company on their behalf.

Privileged access: guarding the keys to the kingdom

Among all accounts in an environment, privileged accounts require the greatest level of protection because they are exactly what attackers seek once they gain an initial foothold. An attacker who compromises an ordinary user account rarely stops there. The next objective is usually *privilege escalation*: gaining administrative access that allows them to disable security controls, move through the network, access sensitive systems, or take control of the environment entirely. For that reason, compromise of a single administrator or root account can quickly become compromise of the organization itself.

This reality is what drives the need for *Privileged Access Management (PAM)*. The idea behind PAM is straightforward: the most powerful accounts should be the hardest to misuse, steal, or expose. Administrative access should not exist permanently simply because it is convenient, nor should highly privileged credentials be casually shared, reused, or left continuously available for attackers to discover.

Instead, organizations try to reduce both the exposure and the lifetime of privileged access. Administrative credentials are often stored in protected vaults where they can be centrally managed and rotated automatically, rather than known permanently by multiple administrators. Likewise, many organizations avoid granting standing administrative access altogether. A user should only receive elevated privileges when needed for a specific task, and only for a limited amount of time. Once the task is complete, those privileges should be removed. This approach limits the opportunity for attackers to steal or abuse powerful accounts that would otherwise remain constantly available.

Because privileged accounts represent such valuable targets, organizations also apply stronger protections to their use than to ordinary accounts. Administrative actions commonly require phishing-resistant multifactor authentication, and privileged sessions are often logged or recorded so that security teams can reconstruct exactly what actions were performed if an incident occurs.

A closely related principle is the separation of administrative identities from ordinary day-to-day user activity. Administrators should not browse the web, read email, or perform routine office work while logged into highly privileged accounts. Everyday user activities are among the most common paths to compromise through phishing attacks, downloading software, malicious attachments, compromised websites, or malware infections. If a privileged account is exposed during those activities, the attacker immediately gains elevated access to critical systems.

For that reason, system administrators typically maintain a separate account for administrative duties and use a standard user account for ordinary work. The privileged account is used only when administrative tasks must be performed on the specific system they are assigned to manage. In practice, this applies the broader principle of least privilege: reducing unnecessary exposure of powerful accounts so that even if one system or user is compromised, it is more difficult for an attacker to gain broader control of the environment

Chapter 6: Firewall Architecture, Deployment, and Networking Foundations

IN THIS CHAPTER

- The firewall as the network's gatekeeper
- A brief networking foundation: what the firewall is actually looking at
- How firewalls evolved, and why it still matters
- Firewall platform architecture: how the box is built
- Form factors: hardware, virtual, and cloud
- Deployment modalities: how a firewall is inserted into the network
- High availability: the firewall must not be a single point of failure
- Network address translation and port address translation
- Firewall logging, management, and sizing in practice
- Security zones: organizing the network for policy

The firewall as the network's gatekeeper

A *firewall* is, at its core, a checkpoint that decides which network traffic may pass and which is blocked, according to a set of rules. It sits at a boundary, between your network and the internet, or between two internal segments, and inspects traffic against its rule set, permitting what is allowed and dropping or rejecting the rest. That single sentence describes everything from a tiny home router to a data-center appliance handling terabits per second, and the rest of this chapter and the next is elaboration on how the idea is built, deployed, and made intelligent. The firewall's enduring value is the enforcement of a simple, ruthless principle: only necessary communication should be possible. If your database server only ever needs to talk to your application servers, a firewall can ensure that nothing else on earth can reach it, and most of a firewall's protective power comes not from blocking exotic attacks but from this disciplined enforcement of "only what is needed," which directly shrinks the attack surface and obstructs the lateral movement that turns a foothold into a catastrophe.

A brief networking foundation: what the firewall is actually looking at

To understand how a firewall makes decisions, you need a working picture of how network traffic is structured, because the firewall reads that structure. Network communication is organized in layers, each adding its own envelope around the data. At the lower layers, traffic is addressed by *IP addresses*, which identify hosts, and divided into *ports*, which identify the particular service on a host, like an apartment number within the building of the address. The combination of source address, source port, destination address, destination port, and protocol is the *five-tuple* that traditionally identifies a connection, and the most basic firewalls make their decisions on exactly these five fields. Above this sits the transport layer, where *TCP* provides reliable, connection-oriented delivery with a recognizable handshake that establishes a session, while *UDP* provides fast, connectionless delivery without one. This distinction matters because a firewall can track the state of a TCP connection in a way it cannot for stateless UDP. Above transport sit the application protocols, such as web, email, file transfer, and thousands of others, which carry the actual content and which a modern firewall increasingly looks into rather than merely past. Knowing this layered structure tells you what each generation of firewall can and cannot see: the older the firewall's design, the lower in the stack it looks and the less it understands about what is actually flowing through it.

How firewalls evolved, and why it still matters

Understanding the generations of firewalls is not history for its own sake; it explains what any given product can and cannot do, and the generations still coexist in real networks. The earliest firewalls were *packet filters*, which judged each packet in isolation by the five-tuple. They were fast but crude, with no memory of context and unable to tell a legitimate reply from an unsolicited probe because they considered each packet alone. *Stateful inspection firewalls* improved on this fundamentally by tracking the state of connections in a table: when an internal host opens an outbound connection, the firewall records it and recognizes the corresponding inbound replies as legitimate, while unsolicited inbound traffic that matches no established connection is suspect by default. Stateful inspection is the baseline expectation for any serious firewall and the foundation on which everything later is built. A related design, the *proxy firewall*, terminates connections on behalf of the protected host and makes its own connection onward, so that the two sides never communicate directly and the proxy can inspect and sanitize the full exchange. This is powerful but heavier, and it is the conceptual ancestor of the decryption proxies discussed two chapters from now. The modern standard is the *next-generation firewall*, which adds the ability to look deep into traffic by identifying the actual application in use rather than just the port, the user behind the traffic rather than just the address, and the content within rather than merely the envelope. The next chapter treats the next-generation firewall in full because its capabilities are the heart of contemporary network defense.

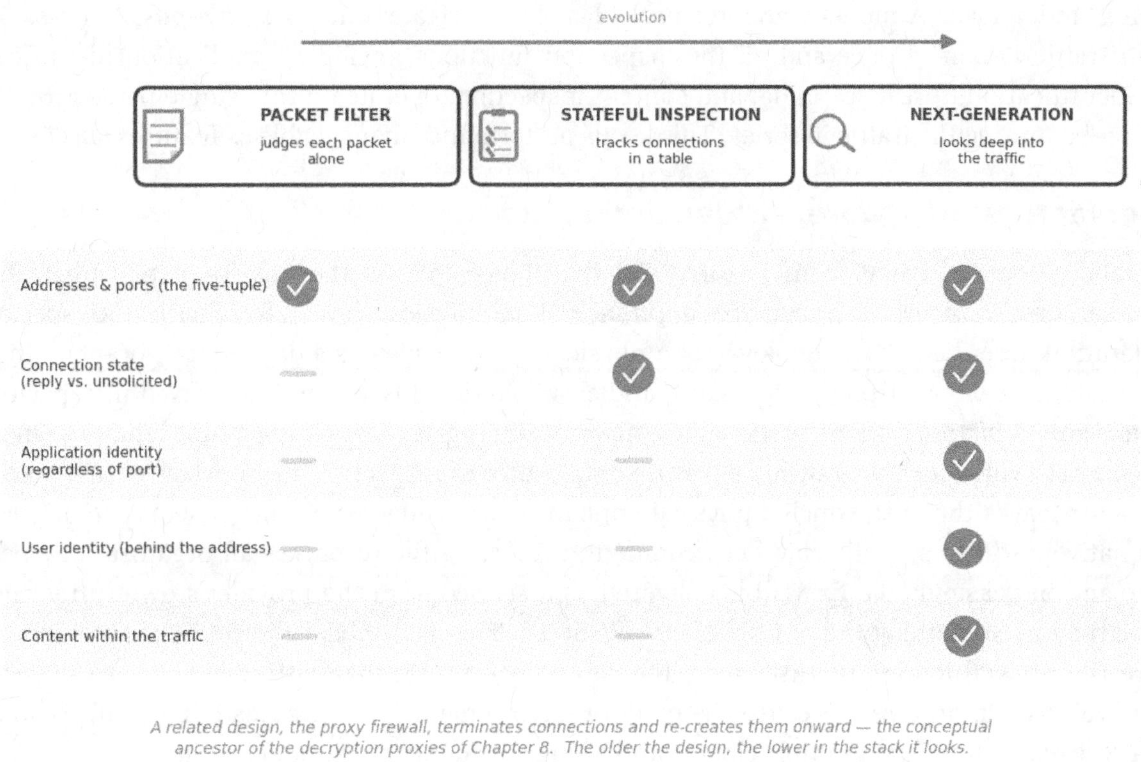

FIGURE 6.1 What each firewall generation can see — the older the design, the lower in the stack it looks.

Firewall platform architecture: how the box is built

It is worth opening the firewall itself, because its internal architecture shapes its performance and its limits. A firewall must do two quite different jobs: it must move packets through at high speed, through the *data plane*, sometimes called the *forwarding plane*, and it must be configured, managed, and monitored, through the *control plane* and *management plane*. Well-designed platforms separate these, so that the heavy lifting of inspecting and forwarding traffic runs on hardware optimized for it while management runs elsewhere. This ensures that a flood of administrative activity or a management fault does not stall the flow of production traffic, and vice versa. The separation also has a security benefit: the management interface, which is a high-value target, can be isolated on its own network away from the data it protects.

The data plane's performance often depends on specialized hardware. General-purpose processors are flexible but comparatively slow at the repetitive, high-volume work of matching packets against rules and scanning content; many firewalls therefore offload that work to *dedicated chips*, purpose-built circuits and accelerators that perform pattern matching, encryption and decryption, and other inspection tasks far faster than general-purpose hardware could. This is why a firewall's headline throughput numbers come with footnotes: a box may forward simple traffic at one rate, inspect application traffic at a lower rate, and decrypt and inspect encrypted traffic at a lower rate still, because each added layer of inspection consumes more of the available processing. Understanding this hierarchy is essential when you size a firewall, because buying for the headline number and then enabling decryption and full inspection is how organizations end up with an expensive appliance gasping under load. A modern architectural idea that mitigates this is *single-pass processing*, in which traffic is parsed once and all the inspection functions, including application identification, user identification, threat scanning, and content inspection, operate on that single parse rather than each re-examining the traffic in series. This keeps performance manageable as features stack up.

Form factors: hardware, virtual, and cloud

Firewalls come in several form factors, and the choice follows the environment rather than a universal best answer. A *hardware appliance* is a physical box, often with the specialized acceleration described above, deployed at a physical location such as a data center, branch office, or campus edge; it offers strong performance and clear physical placement but is fixed in capacity and tied to a site. A *virtual firewall* is the same software running as a virtual machine, deployed wherever virtualization runs, including inside a private data center to inspect traffic between virtual machines that never leaves the host, which a physical appliance at the edge would never see. A *cloud firewall* runs natively within a public cloud environment, protecting the resources an organization operates there, and increasingly the firewall is delivered as a service from the provider's own infrastructure rather than as something the customer installs at all. This is a model the SASE chapter develops, where the firewall follows the user from the cloud edge rather than sitting in any building. Many organizations run all three, because the modern environment is itself spread across physical sites, private virtualization, and multiple clouds, and a single form factor cannot cover it.

Deployment modalities: how a firewall is inserted into the network

How you physically and logically insert a firewall into the traffic path, its *deployment mode*, determines what it can do and how much it disrupts the existing network, and choosing the mode is one of the first decisions in any deployment. In *routed mode*, or *Layer 3 mode*, the firewall acts as a router, with IP addresses on its interfaces, and traffic is routed through it; the firewall is a visible hop in the network and typically also performs address translation and routing decisions. This is the most common and most capable mode, but inserting it means changing the network's routing so that traffic flows through the firewall. In *transparent mode*, or *Layer 2 mode*, sometimes called *bridge mode*, the firewall bridges two segments without IP addresses on its data interfaces and without appearing as a routing hop; it inspects traffic passing through invisibly, which lets you drop a firewall into an existing network with minimal reconfiguration, at the cost of some routing-dependent features. A *virtual wire deployment* is a close cousin, binding two interfaces together so the firewall sits inline inspecting and enforcing policy while being effectively invisible to the surrounding network, useful for inserting enforcement into a path without redesigning it. Finally, *tap mode*, or *passive mode*, connects the firewall to a copy of the traffic, via a network tap or a switch's mirror port, so that it can observe and report on traffic for visibility and tuning without being able to block anything, since it is not in the path. This is invaluable for evaluating what a firewall would do before you commit to letting it enforce. The progression from tap to virtual wire to transparent to routed is roughly a progression from pure observation to full inline control, and a careful rollout often moves along it, starting passive to learn the traffic and tightening to enforcement once the policy is trusted.

High availability: the firewall must not be a single point of failure

Because a firewall sits in the path of traffic, its failure can take an entire site offline, which makes redundancy essential for any deployment that matters. The standard answer is *high availability*, deploying firewalls in pairs or clusters that share state so that one can take over if another fails. In an *active-passive arrangement*, one firewall handles all traffic while its partner stands by, synchronized and ready to assume the load within seconds if the active unit fails; it is simple and predictable but leaves capacity idle. In an *active-active arrangement*, both units pass traffic and share the load, using capacity more fully but adding complexity in keeping their state consistent. The crucial detail in either case is *session synchronization*: the partners continuously share their connection-state tables so that when failover happens, existing connections survive rather than all dropping at once, which would itself be a disruptive event. Designing high availability well means thinking not only about the firewalls but about the surrounding network—the links, the routing, the power—so that the redundancy is genuine and not undone by a shared dependency that fails and takes both firewalls with it..

Network address translation and port address translation

A function intimately bound up with firewalls is *network address translation (NAT)*, which rewrites the IP addresses in traffic as it passes through. NAT exists for two reasons that have become entangled: conserving the limited supply of public internet addresses, and providing a measure of security and flexibility by hiding internal addressing from the outside world. The most common form lets many internal devices, each with a private address that is not routable on the public internet, share one or a few public addresses when communicating outward. Because many internal hosts map to one public address, the firewall must track which internal conversation each returning packet belongs to, and it does this by also translating the port numbers. This is *port address translation (PAT)*, sometimes called *NAT overload*, in which each internal connection is distinguished by a unique combination of the shared public address and a port the firewall assigns. The firewall keeps a translation table mapping these, rewriting addresses and ports outbound and reversing the translation on the replies.

The varieties of NAT are worth distinguishing because they serve different purposes. *Source NAT* translates the source address of outbound traffic, the common case that lets internal users reach the internet from behind a shared public address. *Destination NAT* translates the destination address of inbound traffic, which is how you publish an internal service to the outside world: external users connect to a public address and the firewall redirects them to the private address of the actual server, often called *port forwarding* when only specific ports are redirected. *Static NAT* maps one private address to one public address consistently in both directions, used when a server needs a stable, predictable external presence, while *dynamic NAT* draws from a pool of public addresses as needed. A point that trips up many practitioners is the relationship between NAT and security policy: on most firewalls these are evaluated at different stages, and the security rules may reference the original or the translated addresses depending on the platform's order of operations. Understanding when translation happens relative to when the policy is checked is essential to writing rules that actually match the traffic you intend. A final caution: NAT is sometimes mistaken for a security control in its own right because it hides internal addresses, but obscurity is not security. NAT incidentally complicates an attacker's mapping, but it is the firewall's policy, not the address translation, that actually protects you, and treating NAT as a substitute for real rules is a classic error.

Firewall logging, management, and sizing in practice

A firewall sees an extraordinary amount of what happens on a network, which makes its logs among the richest security data an organization possesses, and treating those logs as a first-class asset rather than an afterthought is part of running a firewall well. A properly configured firewall logs what traffic it allowed and denied, which applications and users it identified, what threats its profiles blocked, what it decrypted, and what URL categories it acted on. This creates a continuous record that feeds directly into the monitoring and correlation of the operations chapter. The practical discipline is to log meaningfully rather than indiscriminately: logging every permitted packet would drown both the firewall and the analyst, so policy typically logs denied traffic, threats, and notable allowed sessions while sampling or summarizing the routine, and forwards all of it to the central logging system so that an attacker who compromises a path cannot erase the evidence by reaching the firewall. The firewall's own reporting, including dashboards of top applications, top users, threats seen, bandwidth consumers, and policy hits, also serves the operational and management purposes the operations chapter describes. It turns raw traffic into a picture of how the network is actually used and attacked, which often reveals both security problems and the stale rules ripe for pruning.

The firewall's management plane deserves protective attention because it is a high-value target: anyone who controls the firewall controls the boundary. Management access should be restricted to a dedicated, isolated network rather than reachable from the general environment or, worse, the internet; it should require strong, phishing-resistant multi-factor authentication and role-based access so that administrators have only the privileges their function requires; and administrative actions should be logged and reviewed, since a malicious or mistaken change to firewall policy can open the whole network silently. Configuration changes belong in the change-management process of the deployment chapter, with review, documentation, and the ability to roll back, and configurations should be backed up so a failed device can be restored from a known-good state under pressure rather than rebuilt from memory.

Finally, sizing and selecting a firewall is a recurring decision that the architecture earlier in this chapter prepares you to make well. The crucial insight is that headline throughput numbers describe the easy case, and real performance falls as inspection deepens: a firewall may forward simple traffic at one rate, apply full application identification and threat inspection at a lower rate, and decrypt and inspect encrypted traffic at a lower rate still, because each layer consumes processing. Sizing for the headline figure and then enabling decryption and full inspection is how organizations end up with an expensive appliance struggling under load and tempting administrators to disable the very inspection they bought it for. Size instead for the realistic traffic mix with the inspection you actually intend to run, including decryption if you plan to decrypt, and leave headroom for growth and for the inevitable expansion of inspection over time. Selection, like every product decision in this book, should lead with the problem: the traffic to be protected, the inspection required, and the environments to be covered. It should not lead with the brand, and it should weigh the full cost of operating the platform, not merely its purchase price, because a firewall poorly tuned or left to decay without updates protects far less than its specifications promise.

Security zones: organizing the network for policy

Modern firewalls organize their interfaces and the networks behind them into *security zones*, named groupings such as "trust" for the internal network, "untrust" for the internet, and "DMZ" for the buffer area that holds internet-facing servers. Zones are not merely labels; they are the unit in which policy is expressed, because rules are written in terms of traffic moving from one zone to another rather than in terms of individual addresses, which makes policy far more readable and maintainable as the network grows. The classic *demilitarized zone (DMZ)* is the most important zone pattern: it holds the systems that must be reachable from the internet, such as web and mail servers, and is isolated so that compromising one of those exposed servers does not put the attacker directly among the internal systems, because traffic from the DMZ to the trusted internal network must itself cross the firewall and satisfy policy. Thinking in zones is the bridge from the raw networking of this chapter to the policy of the next: once the network is divided into zones with clear trust relationships, the firewall's job becomes the explicit, reviewable definition of exactly what traffic may flow between them and what should happen to it along the way. This is precisely the subject we turn to now.

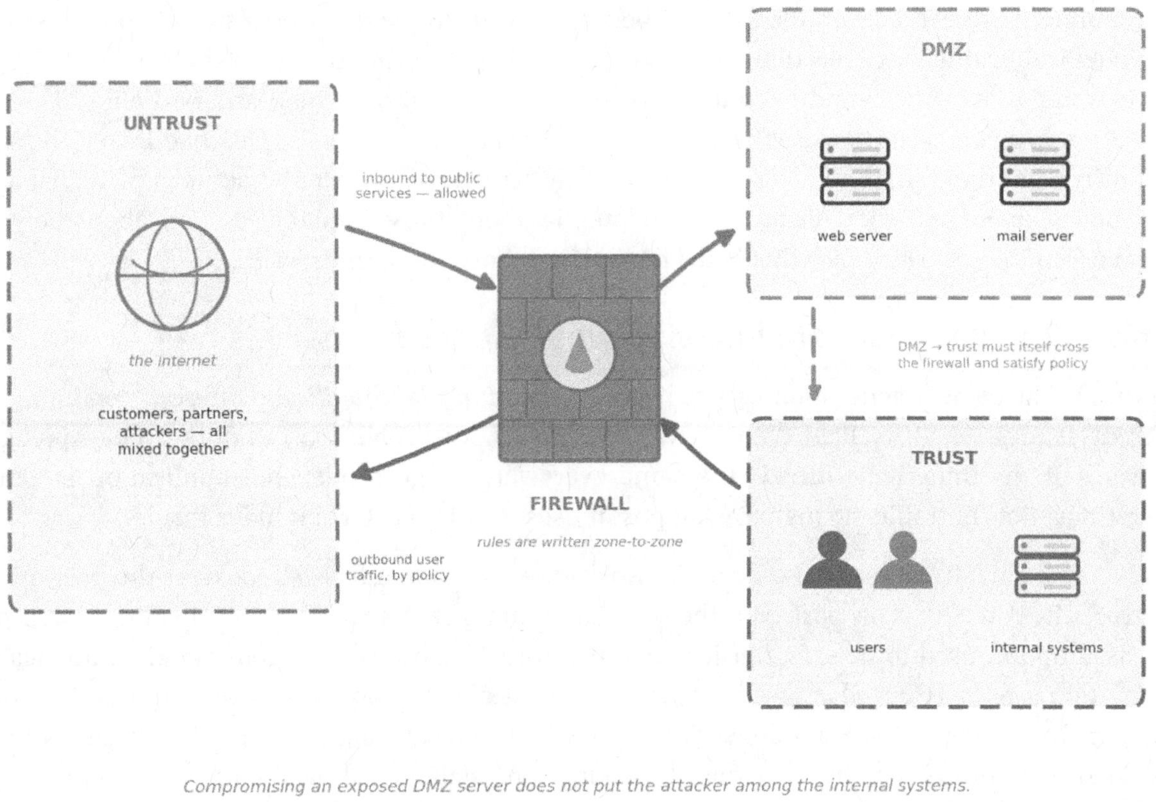

FIGURE 6.2 Security zones and the DMZ — policy is written zone-to-zone, and exposed servers are kept apart from the inside.

Chapter 7: Next-Generation Firewalls — Policy and Traffic Inspection

IN THIS CHAPTER

Beyond ports and addresses

The traditional firewall made its decisions on the five-tuple: addresses, ports, and protocol. For decades this was enough, because services lived on predictable ports and blocking a port reliably blocked the service behind it. That world is gone. Applications now disguise themselves on common ports, tunnel inside other protocols, hop between ports to evade controls, and hide inside the encrypted web traffic that everything uses, so that a rule permitting traffic on the standard web port now permits an enormous and uncontrolled variety of applications, good and bad alike. The *next-generation firewall* exists to close this gap. It does not abandon the five-tuple; it adds to it the ability to identify what the traffic actually is, who is actually sending it, and what it actually contains, and to write policy in those richer terms. This chapter is about those capabilities and about how they combine into the security policy that is the beating heart of a modern firewall.

Application identification: knowing what the traffic really is

The first pillar of next-generation capability is *application identification*. Different vendors give it different names, such as Palo Alto Networks App-ID, Cisco NBAR2, and Fortinet Application Control, but the underlying idea is the same everywhere: figure out what application is actually generating a flow of traffic, no matter what port it uses or what protocol it hides inside.

This is a real shift from how older firewalls worked. A traditional firewall looks at the port number and trusts it. If traffic is on port 443, the firewall assumes it is a web browser loading a web page. That assumption used to be safe, but it is not anymore. Today, an enormous range of applications deliberately uses port 443, because port 443 is almost always allowed out of corporate networks. Dropbox syncing your files, Slack delivering messages, Zoom carrying a video call, a BitTorrent client downloading a movie, a software updater checking for patches, and even malware quietly phoning home to an attacker can all share that same port. The port tells you almost nothing about what is really happening.

So instead of trusting the port, a next-generation firewall looks at the traffic itself and compares what it sees against a library of known applications. The goal is to put a real name on the flow: "this is Microsoft Teams," "this is BitTorrent," "this is a Salesforce session," rather than just "this is traffic on port 443." It does this by layering four techniques together, each one doing a different job.

Deep Packet Inspection

Deep packet inspection is the firewall's ability to look inside the packet, not just at the outside. Think of every packet as an envelope. The outside of the envelope has the addressing information: where the packet came from, where it is going, and which port it is using. A traditional firewall reads only that outside. Deep packet inspection opens the envelope and reads the letter inside. That is all it does at this stage: it gives the firewall access to the contents. It does not yet understand what those contents mean. But without this step, nothing else is possible, because every technique that follows needs to see inside the packet to do its job.

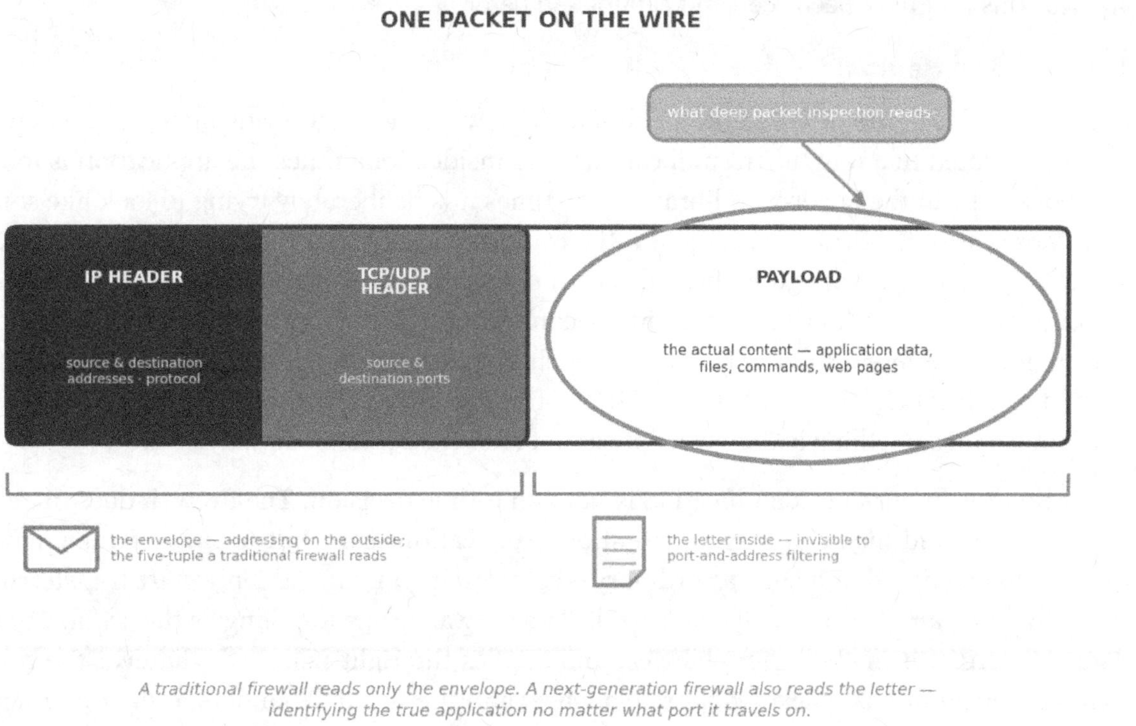

FIGURE 7.1 One packet on the wire — the headers are the envelope; deep packet inspection reads the letter inside.

Protocol Decoding

Protocol decoding is how the firewall makes sense of what is in the envelope. The contents of a packet are written in the "language" of whatever protocol the application uses, such as HTTP for web traffic, TLS for encrypted web traffic, DNS for name lookups, SMTP for email, and so on. The firewall has a built-in reader for each of these languages. When it decodes HTTP, for example, it can pick out which website is being visited and what kind of request is being made. When it decodes TLS, it can read the name of the server the client is trying to reach, even though the rest of the conversation is encrypted. This step is also what lets the firewall catch a common trick: *tunneling*, where someone hides one kind of traffic inside another to sneak it past controls. A file-sharing program might disguise itself as ordinary web traffic, or a remote-access tool might smuggle its commands inside DNS lookups. Because the firewall actually understands what real web traffic and real DNS lookups are supposed to look like, it can spot when something does not fit the pattern and is really a tunnel in disguise.

Signature Matching

Signature matching is pattern recognition. Every well-known application leaves distinctive fingerprints in its traffic: specific text strings, particular ways of formatting its requests, recognizable certificates, and characteristic server names. Security vendors maintain large, constantly updated libraries of these fingerprints, one set per application. When the firewall sees a flow, it checks the fingerprints it has extracted against this library, looking for a match. If the traffic matches the fingerprint for Zoom, the firewall labels the flow as Zoom. If it matches BitTorrent, it labels it as BitTorrent. This is the most direct way to identify an application, and it works well for the thousands of applications that have been seen and catalogued before.

Behavioral and Heuristic

Behavioral and heuristic analysis is the fallback for when no fingerprint matches. Sometimes the traffic is encrypted in a way the firewall cannot read inside. Sometimes the application is too new or too obscure to be in the fingerprint library. Sometimes it is deliberately trying to look like something else. In these cases, the firewall studies how the traffic behaves rather than what it contains. A flow of small, evenly timed packets going both directions looks like a voice or video call, no matter what protocol is carrying it. A flow that opens many connections at once and pulls down large amounts of data from lots of different sources looks like file-sharing, even if the headers have been disguised. By learning the typical rhythms of different kinds of applications, the firewall can make a reasonable guess about what something is even when it cannot read the contents directly.

One last point is important: identification is not a one-time decision. The firewall does not classify a flow at the start and then stop paying attention. Applications can shift behavior in the middle of a session. A connection that begins as ordinary web browsing might suddenly start transferring large files or tunneling another protocol inside itself. The firewall keeps watching as the session continues, updates its verdict if the behavior changes, and applies the right policy to whatever the traffic has become. Every additional packet is more evidence, and the firewall's understanding of a flow stays open until the flow ends.

User identification: knowing who is behind the traffic

The second pillar is *user identification,* which ties network traffic to the actual person or group generating it rather than to the IP address of their device. An IP address is a poor identifier in a modern network: addresses are assigned dynamically and change, a single address may be shared, and a device's address tells you nothing about who is using it or what they are entitled to do. By integrating with the organization's identity systems, including the directory services and authentication infrastructure of the identity chapter, the firewall learns which user is associated with which address at any moment, often by monitoring authentication events, querying the directory, or having users authenticate to the firewall directly. This mapping lets policy be written in terms of users and groups: the finance team may reach the financial application, contractors may reach only a limited set of resources, and an individual under investigation can have their access tightened, all without reference to the shifting addresses of their devices.

User-based policy is transformative for several reasons. It makes rules durable, because they follow the person rather than the address, surviving the constant churn of dynamic addressing. It makes them comprehensible and auditable, because a log that says a named user did something is far more useful in an investigation than one that records only an address that has since been reassigned. It enables least privilege at the network layer, granting each role exactly the network access it needs in language that maps directly to the organization's structure. And it integrates the firewall into the zero-trust posture developed later, where the user's verified identity, not their location on the network, is the basis for what they may reach. Combined with application identification, user identification lets a single rule express something genuinely meaningful: this group of users may use this specific application to reach this zone—and nothing else implied or assumed.

The structure of a security policy

All of this intelligence is marshalled through the firewall's *security policy*, the ordered set of rules that defines what traffic is permitted, what is denied, and what inspection is applied along the way. A security policy is evaluated top to bottom, and the first rule whose criteria match the traffic determines the outcome, which makes rule order consequential: a broad permissive rule placed too high can silently shadow the more specific restrictive rules beneath it, a mistake that quietly opens holes and is among the most common configuration errors in practice. Each rule matches on a combination of criteria, including source and destination zones, source and destination addresses, the identified application, the identified user or group, the service or port, and sometimes the URL category or other attributes. It then specifies an action, most simply allow or deny, but on a modern firewall also which deeper inspection to apply to allowed traffic.

The single most important principle for writing a sound policy is the same *default deny* that has anchored firewalls since the beginning: the policy should permit only what is explicitly intended and deny everything else, ideally with an explicit final rule that denies and logs anything not matched above, so that nothing slips through by oversight and you have a record of what was attempted. The reasoning never changes: you can enumerate what your organization needs far more reliably than you can enumerate every possible threat, so permitting the known-good and denying the rest is the only approach that does not leave you perpetually chasing an infinite list of bads. Beyond default deny, sound policy applies least privilege to each rule, keeping it as narrow as the requirement allows rather than reaching for broad ranges that "just work" and quietly grant far more than intended. It documents each rule with its purpose, requester, and date, so that the policy remains comprehensible and reviewable years later when no one remembers why a rule exists. It is also reviewed regularly to prune the rules that have outlived their purpose, because firewall policies accumulate cruft relentlessly and every stale rule is a potential hole, a lesson the operations chapters return to. A well-built policy reads almost like a description of the business: these users, using these applications, may reach these resources, and everything else is denied and logged.

Security profiles: what happens to the traffic you allow

Permitting traffic is not the same as trusting it. A rule may allow a user to browse the web or use a business application, but the traffic so permitted can still carry malware, exploits, or data leaving the organization. This is the role of *security profiles*, the bundles of deeper inspection that a firewall applies to the traffic a rule has allowed, examining the content for threats even within sanctioned flows. Where the security policy decides whether traffic may pass, security profiles decide what to look for in the traffic that does, and attaching the right profiles to allow rules is what turns a firewall from a traffic cop into an inspector. The common profiles each address a category of threat. *Antivirus and anti-malware inspection* scans permitted traffic for known malicious files and code, blocking the malware that rides along inside otherwise legitimate connections. *Anti-spyware inspection* looks specifically for the command-and-control traffic by which already-installed malware phones home, catching compromise even when the initial infection slipped through. This is a detective control woven into the firewall. *Vulnerability protection*, the firewall's intrusion-prevention function, matches traffic against signatures of known exploits and blocks attempts to exploit vulnerabilities in the systems behind it, providing a shield that buys time when a system cannot be patched immediately. *File blocking* controls which file types may pass in which directions, and *data filtering* watches for sensitive data patterns leaving the organization, a firewall-resident cousin of the data loss prevention discussed later. *URL filtering*, important enough to treat on its own below, governs which web destinations may be reached. The art of profile configuration is balancing thoroughness against performance and false positives: every profile consumes processing and carries some risk of blocking something legitimate, so profiles are tuned to the sensitivity of the traffic, with the heaviest inspection reserved for the flows that matter most.

URL filtering: governing where users may go

URL filtering controls access to web destinations by category and reputation, and it serves both security and acceptable-use goals. The firewall consults a maintained database that classifies web destinations into categories, including malware-hosting sites, phishing pages, command-and-control infrastructure, newly registered domains, and also content categories like gambling or adult material. The policy specifies what to do for each category: block, allow, alert, or warn the user and let them continue. The security value is direct and substantial: blocking access to known-malicious and high-risk categories prevents users from reaching the sites that deliver malware and harvest credentials, and blocking newly registered or uncategorized domains frustrates attackers who stand up fresh infrastructure for each campaign. URL filtering also reinforces the protective-DNS approach discussed in the DNS chapter, the two operating as complementary chokepoints, one resolving names and the other inspecting the connections, so that an attack must evade both. As with every inspection feature, the tuning matters: overly aggressive category blocking generates user friction and help-desk tickets, while a warn-and-continue action for borderline categories preserves productivity while still flagging risk and creating a record. The maintained classification database is what makes URL filtering current rather than a static blocklist, and keeping that intelligence updated is part of the firewall's ongoing care.

Auditing the policy and common configuration mistakes

A security policy is a living document that decays without care, and auditing it is as important as writing it well in the first place. Over time, rules accumulate for projects that ended, employees who left, and servers that were decommissioned, and each *orphaned rule* is a potential hole that no longer serves any purpose but still permits traffic. A disciplined practice reviews the policy on a regular schedule, asking of each rule whether it is still needed, whether it is as narrow as it could be, and whether anyone can still explain why it exists. This is why documenting each rule's purpose, requester, and date at creation pays off years later when the reviewer would otherwise be guessing. Modern platforms assist this by reporting which rules actually match traffic and which have sat unused for months, because a rule that has matched nothing in a year is a strong candidate for removal, and a rule that matches far more than expected may be dangerously broad. Tightening the policy over time, replacing broad rules with narrow ones as you learn the real traffic, removing the unused, and resolving rules that shadow one another, is ongoing work that keeps the firewall's protection from eroding into a permissive sieve.

Several configuration mistakes recur often enough to name explicitly, because recognizing them is half of avoiding them. The most dangerous is the *overly permissive rule*, often a broad "allow" placed high in the policy to make something work quickly, which then shadows the careful restrictive rules beneath it and quietly grants far more than intended. The temporary fix that becomes permanent and forgotten is a classic source of breach. Closely related is *rule ordering gone wrong*, where the top-to-bottom evaluation means a misplaced rule silently overrides others, so that the policy does not do what its author believes. *Any-any rules*, which permit all traffic between broad ranges, defeat the entire purpose of the firewall and yet appear with depressing regularity, sometimes as leftovers from testing. Failing to log denied or notable traffic blinds the organization to what the firewall is seeing and stopping, squandering the rich data the previous section described. Neglecting the *cleanup rule*, the explicit final deny-and-log that catches everything not matched above, leaves the policy's default behavior implicit and unmonitored. And enabling inspection without sizing for it, or letting threat-intelligence subscriptions lapse, leaves a next-generation firewall doing far less than its owners believe, inspecting nothing or matching against stale signatures. The common thread is that a firewall's effectiveness lives in the details of its policy and its upkeep, not in the capability of the box, and the discipline of auditing is what keeps the gap between the two from widening into danger.

Threat intelligence and keeping the firewall current

Several of the capabilities above, including application signatures, exploit signatures, malware identification, and URL classification, depend on maintained intelligence that is only as good as its currency. A next-generation firewall is therefore not a static device but a subscriber to continuously updated feeds of *threat intelligence*, signatures, and classifications, and a firewall whose subscriptions have lapsed or whose updates have stalled is steadily decaying toward the crude port-and-address device of decades past, blind to everything discovered since it last updated. Keeping these feeds current is as essential to a firewall's effectiveness as patching is to a server's, and it belongs in the same operational discipline. Modern platforms also share intelligence across an installed base, so that a threat identified at one organization can inform protections everywhere within minutes. This is a genuine advantage of the cloud-connected model, though one that, like all such models, trades some independence for the benefit of collective defense.

Putting policy and inspection together

It is worth assembling the pieces into the single coherent decision a modern firewall makes for a flow of traffic. The traffic arrives and is associated with its source and destination zones. The firewall identifies the true application regardless of port, and identifies the user behind it by reference to the identity systems. It evaluates the security policy top to bottom, matching on zones, addresses, application, user, and service, and finds the first rule that applies. If that rule denies, the traffic is dropped and logged. If it allows, the firewall applies the security profiles attached to that rule, scanning for malware and exploits, checking the URL category, watching for sensitive data and disallowed file types, and permits the traffic only insofar as it survives that inspection, logging throughout. All of this, on a well-architected platform, happens in a single pass at line rate, fast enough that the user never notices, and the result is enforcement expressed in the meaningful language of users and applications rather than the brittle language of ports and addresses. This is what a next-generation firewall does, and understanding it as one integrated decision rather than a pile of features is what lets you configure it well. One layer remains, however, that everything above quietly depends on: the firewall can only inspect what it can read, and the overwhelming majority of modern traffic is encrypted, which is the subject of the next chapter.

Chapter 8: Decrypting and Inspecting Encrypted Traffic

IN THIS CHAPTER

The inspection blind spot
What encrypted traffic hides, and the risk it carries
How decryption works: the firewall as a controlled intermediary
The hard parts: privacy, legality, trust, and breakage
Certificate management and the mechanics of inspection
Deciding whether and how to decrypt

The inspection blind spot

The previous chapter described a firewall that identifies applications, scans for malware, blocks exploits, and watches for data leaving the organization. Almost all of that capability depends on the firewall being able to read the traffic—yet the overwhelming majority of internet traffic today is encrypted with *TLS*, the same transport encryption that protects your banking session. For confidentiality, this is an enormous and welcome victory: the web that once sent passwords and personal data in the clear now encrypts nearly everything by default. But it creates a profound problem for network defense, because encryption is indifferent to intent. It protects the attacker's malware download and command-and-control channel exactly as faithfully as it protects your customer's login. To the firewall, encrypted traffic is opaque: the stream of ciphertext reveals only its outer envelope of addresses. The deep packet inspection described in the previous chapter is blind to it, unless the firewall can somehow see inside. This chapter is about how organizations restore that visibility, what it costs, and what it means.

What encrypted traffic hides, and the risk it carries

It is worth being precise about the security problem, because it is easy to underrate. When traffic is encrypted end to end, the firewall can still see the addresses involved and can often glean the destination site's name from the early, still-readable part of the connection setup. From this limited outside view, it can make some decisions, such as blocking connections to known-malicious destinations, which is why URL and reputation filtering work to a degree even without decryption. But it cannot see the content: it cannot scan the encrypted file transfer for malware, cannot detect the exploit hidden in the encrypted web request, cannot identify the application tunneling inside the encrypted session, and cannot notice the sensitive database quietly leaving the organization inside an encrypted upload.

Attackers understand this perfectly and exploit it deliberately. A large and growing share of malware delivery, command-and-control communication, and data exfiltration now rides inside encryption precisely because it defeats inspection, hiding in the same protective wrapper that legitimate traffic uses. The uncomfortable consequence is that an organization which encrypts everything for confidentiality but inspects nothing has, without realizing it, blinded its own defenses. The very controls it paid for, scanning for malware and exploits and data loss, are looking at ciphertext and seeing nothing. This is the central risk of encrypted traffic from a defender's standpoint: not that encryption is bad, but that it is morally neutral, and the defender who does not account for it is defending only the shrinking fraction of traffic that remains readable.

How decryption works: the firewall as a controlled intermediary

To inspect encrypted traffic, the firewall must become a controlled intermediary that decrypts the traffic, inspects it, and re-encrypts it before sending it on. This technique is generally called *TLS inspection* or *SSL decryption*, and architecturally it is a man-in-the-middle performed deliberately and with authority by the organization on its own traffic. The mechanism rests directly on the public key infrastructure of the encryption chapter. Recall that a client trusts a website because the site presents a certificate signed by a chain leading back to a certificate authority the client already trusts.

In TLS inspection, the firewall interposes itself. When an internal user initiates an encrypted connection outward, the firewall intercepts it, makes its own encrypted connection to the real destination, and presents back to the user a certificate that the firewall generates on the fly for that destination. That certificate is signed by an internal certificate authority that the organization has installed as trusted on all its managed devices. Because the devices trust the organization's internal authority, they accept the firewall's substitute certificate without complaint, and the user's browser shows a normal secure connection.

The firewall now sits in the middle holding both halves. It decrypts the traffic from the user, inspects the now-readable content with all the profiles of the previous chapter, and re-encrypts it onward to the real destination, doing the same in reverse for the replies. The decryption is transient and in memory, the same disciplined, in-use handling the encryption chapter described, and the traffic is re-encrypted before it continues. But for the moment of inspection, the firewall can see and act on everything.

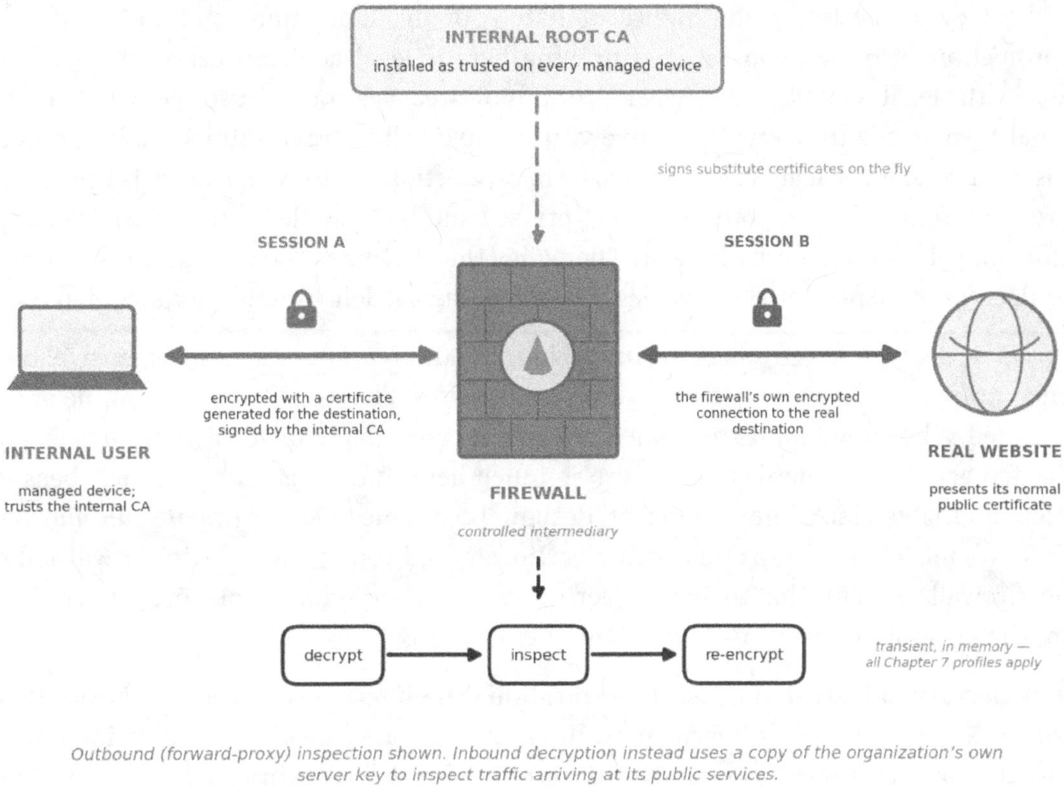

FIGURE 8.1 TLS inspection — the firewall as a controlled intermediary holding both halves of the encrypted conversation.

There are two broad directions of inspection, and they solve different problems. *Outbound decryption*, or *forward-proxy decryption*, inspects the traffic of internal users connecting to external sites. This is the case above, and it is what lets you scan your users' web and application traffic for malware, exploits, and data loss even though it is encrypted. *Inbound decryption* inspects traffic arriving from the internet to servers the organization itself operates, such as its public web applications. Here, the firewall holds a copy of the server's own private key and certificate, so it can decrypt the inbound connections to the server and inspect them for attacks against that server before they arrive. The outbound case protects users from the outside world; the inbound case protects the organization's own services from attackers. Most organizations that decrypt do both, applying each where it fits.

The hard parts: privacy, legality, trust, and breakage

Decryption is powerful, and it is also the most fraught capability in this book, because it deliberately breaks the privacy guarantee that encryption exists to provide. The considerations are not merely technical, and a professional who deploys decryption without weighing them is courting both harm and liability. The most serious is privacy and trust: by decrypting, the organization can read the content of its users' encrypted sessions, which is exactly the capability that surveillance abuses, and which carries real legal and ethical weight that varies by jurisdiction and by the relationship between the organization and the people whose traffic it inspects.

Inspecting the traffic of employees on corporate devices is one thing, generally permissible with clear notice and policy. Inspecting traffic indiscriminately, or in jurisdictions and contexts with strong privacy protections, can be unlawful, and nothing here is legal advice. Decryption policy must be developed with legal counsel and clear, communicated acceptable-use policy. The standard professional response is to decrypt selectively, not universally. Organizations maintain *decryption exclusions* that exempt sensitive categories from inspection entirely, such as traffic to banking, healthcare, and financial sites, both to respect privacy and because the legal exposure of decrypting such traffic outweighs the security benefit. The policy thus becomes “decrypt and inspect by default, but never decrypt these protected categories,” a balance struck deliberately and documented.

Beyond privacy, decryption introduces technical hazards. It is computationally expensive; decrypting and re-encrypting traffic is among the heaviest things a firewall does. This is why, as the architecture chapter warned, a box sized for its headline throughput can collapse once decryption is enabled, and why dedicated acceleration hardware matters so much here. It can also break things, because some applications and sites resist interception by design. Techniques like *certificate pinning*, where an application is built to trust only one specific certificate and reject any substitute, will fail outright when the firewall presents its generated certificate, so decryption deployments require careful exclusion of such applications to avoid breaking them.

Decryption also expands trust and risk concentration. The internal certificate authority that makes decryption possible is an extraordinarily powerful secret anyone who steals it could impersonate any website to the organization’s devices. The decrypting firewall also briefly holds the plaintext of everything it inspects, making it a concentrated, high-value target whose compromise would be severe. Finally, decryption interacts awkwardly with certificate validation, since the firewall must itself rigorously validate the certificates of the real destinations on the users’ behalf. The users can no longer do so themselves; they see only the firewall’s substitute certificate. If the firewall fails to check the real site’s certificate properly, it has stripped away the very protection the users believe they have.

Certificate management and the mechanics of inspection

The practical heart of decryption is *certificate management*, and getting it right is what separates a deployment that works invisibly from one that floods users with browser warnings and breaks applications. Recall that inspection depends on the firewall presenting, for each site a user visits, a freshly generated certificate signed by an internal certificate authority that the organization’s devices trust. For this to work silently, that internal authority’s certificate must be distributed to and trusted by every managed device, usually pushed out through device-management tooling so that browsers and applications accept the firewall’s substitute certificates without complaint. The moment a device lacks that trusted internal authority, the user sees alarming security warnings, because their browser is correctly reporting that the certificate it received is not one it trusts. This is the most common operational stumble in decryption rollouts, and it appears immediately on any device the distribution missed, such as a personal phone, a contractor’s laptop, or an unmanaged server.

The *internal certificate authority* that makes all this possible is among the most dangerous secrets the organization holds, because whoever controls it can impersonate any website to every device that trusts it. It therefore warrants the strongest protection available, ideally generated and held within a *hardware security module* so the private key never leaves protected hardware, with tightly controlled access and careful logging, exactly the key-management rigor the encryption chapter demanded for crown-jewel keys.

A subtler obligation falls on the firewall during inspection. Because the user can no longer see or validate the real destination's certificate, and instead sees only the firewall's substitute, the firewall must rigorously validate the genuine site's certificate on the user's behalf. That means checking its chain, expiration, and revocation, and refusing or warning when the real certificate is invalid. A decryption deployment that neglects this has silently stripped away the very protection users believe they still enjoy, presenting a reassuring lock icon for connections to sites whose certificates the firewall never actually checked. Handling these mechanics well, including distributing trust to every device, guarding the internal authority absolutely, validating destination certificates faithfully, and maintaining the exclusions that keep sensitive and pinned traffic out of inspection entirely, is the difference between decryption that quietly restores visibility and decryption that breaks things and exposes the organization to new risk.

Deciding whether and how to decrypt

Given all this, whether to decrypt is a genuine risk decision in the sense of the risk chapter, weighing the substantial security benefit of restoring inspection against real costs in privacy, performance, complexity, and concentrated risk. For many organizations, the security benefit is decisive: the inability to inspect the majority of traffic is a gap attackers actively exploit, and the controls already purchased are largely wasted without it. But the decision should be made consciously and implemented carefully rather than flipped on as a default.

A sound deployment decrypts selectively with well-maintained exclusions for sensitive and privacy-protected categories; protects the internal certificate authority with the rigor of any crown-jewel secret, ideally in a hardware module; sizes the firewall for the real load that decryption imposes rather than the headline number; validates destination certificates rigorously on users' behalf; excludes applications that cannot tolerate interception; and rests on clear, communicated policy developed with legal counsel so that the people whose traffic is inspected know it and the organization stands on firm ground.

Done this way, decryption restores the visibility on which the rest of network defense depends. Done carelessly, it breaks applications, exposes the organization to legal and ethical hazard, and concentrates a dangerous new risk. The capability is neither to be avoided nor to be deployed casually, and knowing the difference is exactly the judgment this book is meant to build.

Chapter 9: Intrusion Prevention, VPNs, and Data Loss Prevention

IN THIS CHAPTER

The firewall, however capable, is one component among several that share the work of network defense. This chapter covers three more: intrusion detection and prevention, virtual private networks, and data loss prevention. These interlock with the firewall and with each other as layers of a single design. On a modern platform, several of these may be functions of the firewall itself rather than separate boxes, but the concepts are distinct and worth understanding in their own right, because each addresses a failure mode the others do not.

Intrusion detection and prevention

Prevention is never complete. Some attacks get through, whether through a novel technique, a misconfiguration, a permitted-but-malicious flow, or a legitimate-looking action by a compromised account. This is why detection is not optional. An *intrusion detection system* watches for signs that an attack is underway or has succeeded so that you can respond, while an *intrusion prevention system* goes further and actively blocks the malicious traffic it detects. The distinction is a smoke detector versus a sprinkler: detection notices and raises the alarm, while prevention notices and responds automatically. Each has its place. Detection-only is safer where a false positive that blocks legitimate traffic would be costly, since a wrong alarm is merely noise rather than an outage, while prevention suits cases where the speed of automated blocking outweighs the risk of occasionally stopping something legitimate. Many real deployments run in prevention mode for high-confidence signatures and detection mode for lower-confidence heuristics, getting automatic protection where they trust it and human review where they do not.

There are two fundamental ways these systems decide what is suspicious, and understanding both explains their strengths and their maddening limitations. *Signature-based detection* looks for patterns known to indicate specific attacks: the digital fingerprint of a particular exploit or piece of malware. It is precise and produces few false alarms for the threats it knows, but it is blind by definition to anything new. An attack with no existing signature sails straight past, which is why signatures must be constantly updated and why they cannot be the only line. *Anomaly-based detection* takes the opposite approach, learning what normal looks like for an environment and flagging significant deviations from it. Its great advantage is the ability to catch novel attacks that have no signature, because it reacts to unusual rather than to known-bad. Its weakness is the mirror image, since "unusual" and "malicious" are not the same thing, so anomaly detection generates more false positives and requires patient tuning to your environment lest legitimate change drown you in alerts. The mature answer uses both: signatures catch the known cheaply and quietly, anomaly detection provides a chance against the unknown, and the combination feeding into the monitoring systems of the operations chapter is far stronger than either alone.

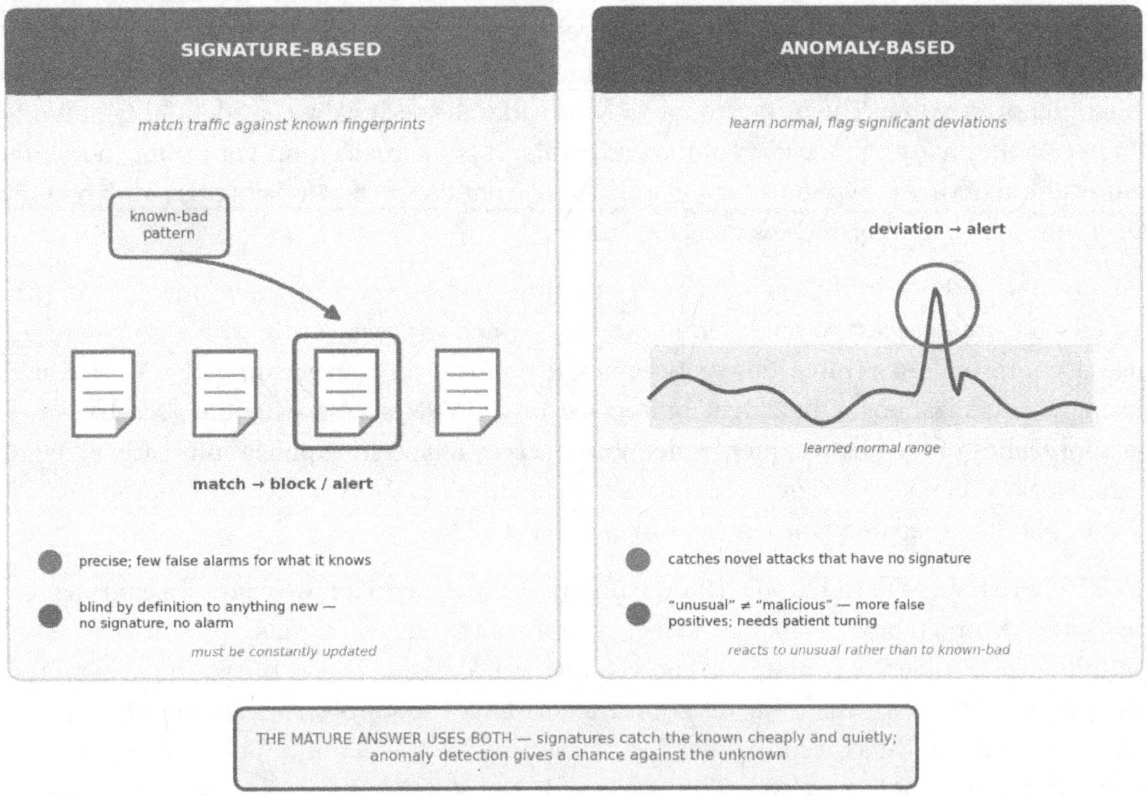

FIGURE 9.1 Signature-based and anomaly-based detection — precise against the known versus a chance against the unknown.

These systems watch at two vantage points, and good coverage wants both. A *network-based sensor* watches traffic crossing the network, giving broad visibility into communications between systems and a good chance of spotting scanning, lateral movement, and command-and-control traffic. A *host-based sensor* lives on an individual machine and watches what happens there, including file changes, process behavior, and local logs. This gives deep visibility into a single host that network sensors cannot match, including activity that never crosses the network or that would be encrypted in transit. The network sensor sees the forest; the host sensor sees the tree in detail. Modern endpoint defense has evolved this host-based idea into *endpoint detection and response*, which continuously records detailed endpoint activity and enables both automated response and after-the-fact investigation. It has evolved further into platforms that correlate signals across endpoints, network, and cloud, extending the same principle that more vantage points, correlated, beat any single one.

Virtual private networks

A *virtual private network* creates an encrypted tunnel across an untrusted network so that traffic passing through it is protected from eavesdropping and tampering, and so that a remote system can be treated, within limits, as if it were on a trusted network. The two dominant uses are *remote access*, where individual employees connect securely to organizational resources from wherever they are, and *site-to-site connections*, where two locations are linked over the public internet as though they shared a private line. The protection a VPN provides is specifically confidentiality and integrity of data in transit, plus authentication of the endpoints. It is the realization, for remote and inter-site communication, of the encryption-in-transit principle from the encryption chapter, built on the same hybrid cryptography and certificates described there.

The role of the VPN is shifting, and honesty requires saying so. The traditional model grants a connected user broad access to the internal network, which sits awkwardly with zero-trust thinking, because a compromised remote device becomes a doorway into everything the VPN can reach. Increasingly, organizations supplement or replace broad VPN access with the zero-trust network access approaches of the next chapter, which grant access to specific applications rather than to the whole network. When you design remote access today, the question is therefore not merely "which VPN," but "should broad network access be the model at all."

Where a VPN remains the right tool, sound configuration rests on a few pillars. Use strong, current protocols and cryptography, disabling the legacy options that linger in many products for backward compatibility, since older VPN protocols carry known weaknesses. This is the practical application of the encryption chapter's insistence on sound algorithms. Require strong authentication, ideally phishing-resistant multi-factor authentication, because a VPN credential is a key to your network and protecting it with only a password invites exactly the stolen-credential attacks that multi-factor authentication defeats. Constrain what the VPN grants, applying least privilege so a connected user or site reaches only the resources actually needed rather than the entire internal network, which limits the damage if an endpoint is compromised. Finally, decide deliberately how the tunnel handles other traffic. Routing all of a remote user's traffic through the organization gives visibility and control but consumes bandwidth, while routing only organization-bound traffic is lighter but sees less.

On maintenance, VPNs demand the same care as firewalls and for a sharper reason: VPN gateways are high-value, internet-facing targets, and several of the most damaging breaches of recent years began with an unpatched VPN appliance that gave an attacker a foothold straight into the network. Keep the concentrators and client software patched promptly. Review access regularly and revoke credentials and certificates for departed employees and ended projects, since a stale VPN account is a quiet back door. Manage certificates and keys through their lifecycle so nothing expires unexpectedly or lingers past its safe life. Feed VPN logs into the monitoring pipeline, because a login from an implausible location or at an impossible hour is exactly the anomaly that signals a compromised credential.

How a VPN tunnel is actually built: IPsec and TLS VPNs

It is worth opening the VPN to see how the encrypted tunnel is actually constructed, because the two dominant approaches have different strengths that shape where each is used. The traditional foundation of site-to-site and many remote-access VPNs is *IPsec*, a suite of protocols that secures traffic at the network layer, beneath the applications, so that everything flowing between the endpoints is protected without the applications needing to know. IPsec works in two phases that echo the hybrid cryptography of the encryption chapter. In the first phase, the two endpoints authenticate each other using certificates or a shared secret, and establish a secure channel using asymmetric techniques and a Diffie-Hellman key exchange, much like the TLS handshake. In the second phase, they use that channel to agree on the symmetric keys and parameters that will protect the actual traffic, and then bulk data flows encrypted and integrity-protected between them. Because IPsec operates at the network layer and protects everything transparently, it is the natural choice for linking whole sites together. Its keys are periodically renegotiated so that a compromise has a limited window, building the key-rotation hygiene urged in the encryption chapter into the protocol itself.

The other major approach builds the VPN on *TLS*, the same protocol that secures the web. This gives it a significant practical advantage for remote access: because TLS traffic looks like ordinary secure web traffic and travels over the same ports, a TLS-based VPN passes through restrictive networks and firewalls that might block IPsec, which makes it convenient for users connecting from arbitrary locations like hotels and client sites. *TLS VPNs* often deliver access to specific applications through a browser or a lightweight client, which aligns naturally with the per-application, least-privilege direction that zero-trust network access carries further.

In choosing between them, the trade-offs are real. IPsec is robust and efficient for connecting networks and protecting all traffic transparently, while TLS-based remote access is flexible, traverses hostile networks more easily, and lends itself to granular, application-level access. Many organizations use both: IPsec to stitch their sites together, TLS-based access for roaming users, and increasingly the zero-trust access of the architecture chapter layered over or in place of the broad-access remote VPN. Whichever is used, the configuration principles already stated hold: strong current cryptography with legacy options disabled, strong multi-factor authentication on the endpoints, least-privilege scoping of what the tunnel reaches, and diligent patching of the gateways that, as repeatedly warned, are among the most attacked devices an organization exposes.

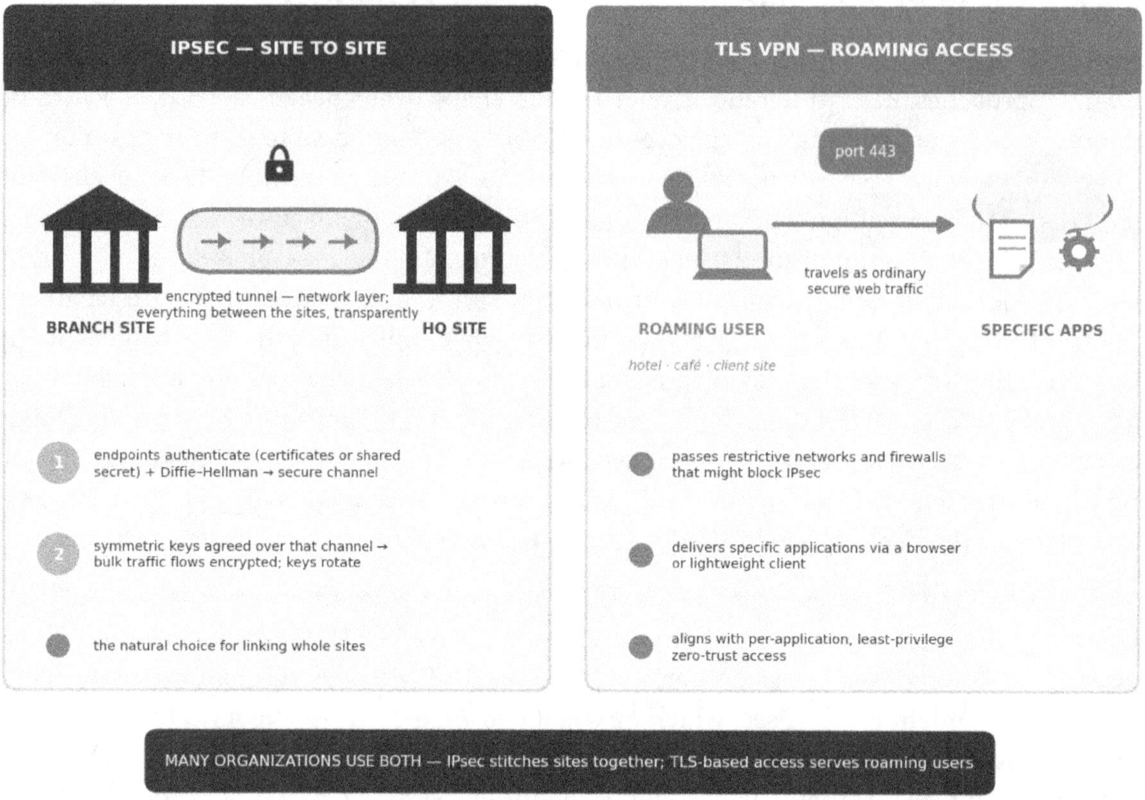

FIGURE 9.2 IPsec and TLS VPNs — the two ways the encrypted tunnel is actually built, and where each fits.

Data loss prevention

Where the other tools mostly keep attackers out or detect them once inside, *data loss prevention* addresses a different question: how do you stop sensitive data from leaving where it should not? The threat it answers includes both the malicious insider deliberately exfiltrating data and, more commonly, the negligent insider who emails the wrong file, uploads confidential material to a personal cloud account, or copies records to a removable drive without ill intent. A data loss prevention system identifies sensitive data and then monitors and controls its movement, operating at several points: on the network, watching data in transit for sensitive content leaving the organization; on endpoints, controlling what can be copied to removable media, printed, or uploaded; and in storage, scanning to discover where sensitive data resides, which often surfaces copies in places nobody intended. Its effectiveness depends entirely on the data classification of the assets chapter, because the system can only protect what it has been taught to recognize as sensitive, whether by matching patterns such as the formats of payment cards or identification numbers, by recognizing fingerprints of specific documents, or by reading classification labels applied to the data.

It is important to set expectations honestly, both for yourself and for the executives you advise, because data loss prevention is routinely oversold. It is very effective against accidental and casual loss: the misaddressed email, the careless upload, and similar mistakes. Since most data-loss incidents are mistakes rather than malice, this addresses the bulk of real-world cases. It is far less effective against a determined, knowledgeable insider, who can often find a path it does not cover, particularly if they can transform the data into a form the system does not recognize, encrypt it before it leaves, or simply photograph the screen. Presenting data loss prevention as a complete defense against insider theft oversells it badly; presenting it as a strong reduction of the most common forms of leakage, plus a deterrent and detector for the rest, is accurate.

The capability also interacts directly with the encrypted-traffic problem of the previous chapter: network-based data loss prevention can only inspect traffic it can read, so without decryption it is blind to sensitive data leaving inside encrypted uploads. This is one more reason the decryption decision ripples through the whole architecture. Data loss prevention also carries operational cost worth naming: it can be intrusive, occasionally blocking legitimate work and generating false positives that frustrate users and bury analysts, and it requires careful tuning and clear policy about what is sensitive and what should happen on a violation. The response may be to block outright, warn the user, or quietly log for review. That is a real trade-off between protection and friction, and it should be made consciously for each category of data rather than set once and forgotten.

Chapter 10: Zero Trust, Microsegmentation, SASE, and SD-WAN

IN THIS CHAPTER

Zero trust: never trust, always verify

The erosion of the old inside-outside model, noted throughout this book, demands a new organizing principle, and that principle is *zero trust*. Its slogan, "never trust, always verify," captures the core shift: no user or device is trusted merely because of where it sits on the network. The traditional castle-and-moat design granted broad trust to anything inside the walls, which meant that an attacker who breached the perimeter, or an insider already inside it, could move freely toward the valuable systems. Zero trust rejects implicit trust based on network location and instead requires that every access request be authenticated, authorized, and verified against context before it is granted, regardless of where it originates. A request from inside the office is treated with the same scrutiny as one from a café across the world.

Three principles structure the model. *Verify explicitly*: every request is authenticated and authorized using all available signals, including identity, device health, location, behavior, and the sensitivity of what is being accessed, rather than assumed safe because of its origin. *Use least-privilege access*: grant the minimum needed for the specific task, for the shortest sensible time, narrowing what any single compromise can reach. *Assume breach*: design and operate as though an attacker is already inside, which leads naturally to segmenting aggressively, encrypting everywhere, monitoring continuously, and limiting the blast radius of any compromise. In practice, realizing zero trust leans heavily on the identity foundations of the identity chapter, especially strong, phishing-resistant authentication and fine-grained authorization, combined with *device-posture checks* that assess whether the connecting device is healthy and managed, and a *policy engine* that makes a contextual decision for each access request rather than granting standing access. It is less a product you buy than an architecture you move toward, almost always incrementally over years. The fact that vendors sell "zero trust products" should not obscure that it is fundamentally a strategy and a posture, assembled from many of the controls this book describes rather than purchased in a box. The canonical reference for the model is NIST's zero-trust architecture guidance, SP 800-207, noted among the domain frameworks of the risk chapter, which gives this posture structured form rather than leaving it a slogan. Because the move toward it is gradual, the CISA Zero Trust Maturity Model, also noted there, is the practical companion for assessing how far along that road an organization actually is across its identity, device, network, application, and data pillars, and for planning the next increment.

Segmentation and microsegmentation

A concrete and long-standing expression of "assume breach" is *segmentation*: dividing the network into separate zones with controlled connections between them, so that compromise in one zone does not grant the run of the whole environment. The reasoning follows directly from the anatomy of an attack: adversaries rely on lateral movement, and a flat network where everything can talk to everything is an attacker's paradise because one foothold leads everywhere. Segmentation forces an attacker to cross controlled, monitored boundaries to reach what they want, giving you both barriers to slow them and chokepoints to detect them. Classic segmentation separates systems by sensitivity and function, with internet-facing servers in the DMZ, user workstations in one internal zone, and sensitive databases in a tightly restricted other. Firewalls enforce that only necessary traffic crosses, exactly the zone-based policy of the firewall chapters applied to internal structure rather than only the perimeter.

Microsegmentation pushes this idea to its logical conclusion. Rather than a handful of large zones, the network is divided very finely, often down to the level of individual workloads or applications, with policy controlling communication between each small segment and every other. The aim is to shrink the blast radius of any compromise to the smallest possible area, so that an attacker who lands on one machine finds it can talk to almost nothing else without crossing a policy boundary that both blocks and logs the attempt. Microsegmentation directly embodies the assume-breach mindset by treating even internal, machine-to-machine, *east-west traffic* as something to be verified rather than trusted, closing the lateral pathways that flat networks leave wide open. It is more demanding to implement and operate than coarse segmentation because it requires understanding which workloads legitimately need to talk to which, and that is often poorly documented. It is frequently realized in software rather than physical firewalls, with policy enforced at each workload or host so that the segmentation follows the workload even as it moves between servers or clouds. The payoff is that the inevitable initial compromise stays contained to a single workload rather than spreading, which is precisely the outcome the whole assume-breach philosophy is built to achieve.

SASE: security delivered from the cloud edge

The same forces that dissolved the network perimeter, cloud adoption and remote work, also broke the old way of delivering security. In the traditional model, security controls lived in the corporate data center, and remote users' traffic was hauled, or backhauled, all the way back to headquarters to be inspected before going out to the internet or the cloud. This was a wasteful detour that added latency and made little sense once the applications themselves had moved to the cloud and the users had moved out of the office. *Secure Access Service Edge (SASE)*, pronounced "sassy," is the architectural answer: it converges networking and security into a single service delivered from the cloud, at *points of presence* distributed close to wherever users actually are, so that protection follows the user rather than living in a building they no longer visit. Traffic goes to the nearest cloud point of presence, is inspected and secured there, and proceeds to its destination, with the user's policy applied consistently whether they sit in headquarters, at home, or in an airport. Because the whole bundle is delivered as a single cloud service, administrators manage one set of policies from one console rather than juggling separate appliances and management tools for each capability.

SASE bundles several capabilities that were once separate appliances, and it is worth naming each because they are often discussed individually. The networking half is *software-defined* ***wide-area networking*, treated on its own below. The security half, often sold separately as the *Security Service Edge (SSE)* when an organization wants the security capabilities without changing its networking, comprises several parts: a *secure web gateway* that filters and inspects web traffic for threats and enforces acceptable use, performing in the cloud the URL filtering and content inspection the firewall chapters described; a *cloud access security broker*, treated below, which governs the use of cloud applications; *zero trust network access*, which operates on the principle of "never trust, always verify" by checking the user's identity, the device they are using, and the context of the request on every connection, and which grants the user access to specific applications rather than to the whole network; and *firewall as a service*, which delivers the firewall capabilities of the earlier chapters from the cloud rather than from an appliance on premises. Most SASE platforms also fold in data-loss-prevention and DNS-layer security capabilities, both important enough to merit their own sections later in this book. The thread tying all of these together is that security is applied at the edge, near the user, as a continuously updated cloud service, rather than backhauled to a central chokepoint or pinned to hardware in a particular building.**

SD-WAN: the networking half

Software-defined wide-area networking (SD-WAN) is the networking foundation that SASE builds on, and it deserves understanding in its own right because it solved a real problem before security converged onto it.

To see what that problem was, it helps to picture the older model SD-WAN replaced. For a long time, organizations ran their networks so that every branch office sent all of its traffic back to a central data center first. Whether an employee was opening an internal company system or just watching a video on the open internet, the traffic was hauled to headquarters, inspected and managed there, and then sent back out. The connections that carried this traffic were expensive, rigid private circuits, and the routing decisions were tied to fixed hardware configurations at each site. This made sense when the important applications lived inside the data center. It made much less sense once those applications moved to the cloud and employees started working from everywhere, because the network was now dragging traffic to headquarters just to send it right back out to a cloud service somewhere else.

SD-WAN changes this by abstracting the network control into software, so each site can make smart routing decisions on its own, guided by central policy. It typically has more than one kind of connection available to it: ordinary broadband internet, the same cable, fiber, or DSL service a home user might have; cellular links like 4G or 5G for wireless backup or for sites where wiring is impractical; and *MPLS*, a private circuit leased from a carrier that does not travel over the public internet. MPLS is generally the most reliable and predictable option, but it is also the most expensive, while broadband is cheap and plentiful but shares the public internet with everyone else. Rather than forcing all traffic onto one of these, SD-WAN looks at what each flow needs and picks the right path for it. A user streaming Netflix does not need to go through the corporate data center and does not need an expensive private circuit; SD-WAN can send that traffic straight out over broadband. A connection to an internal financial system, on the other hand, can be steered over the MPLS link, where it is more private and more reliable. The decisions are made automatically, in real time, based on policies that an administrator sets once from a central management console rather than configuring each branch router by hand. The result is better performance and resilience, since traffic can also fail over between links automatically if one connection degrades, and far simpler operations, since policy is managed from one place rather than configured box by box.

The connection to SASE is natural and was almost inevitable. Once the network is controlled in software and traffic is being steered intelligently, applying security to that traffic at the cloud edge as it is steered becomes the obvious next step. SD-WAN plus cloud-delivered security is precisely what SASE is.

CASB: governing the cloud applications people actually use

The *cloud access security broker (CASB)* addresses a problem that the firewall and VPN were never designed for: the sprawling use of cloud applications, sanctioned and unsanctioned, that defines modern work. Employees adopt cloud services constantly, often without involving the IT department at all. This is the phenomenon of *shadow IT*, in which a team starts using some cloud tool to get its work done and the organization has data sitting in a service it does not even know about. A CASB sits between users and cloud services, whether as a proxy in the traffic path or by connecting directly to the cloud services' own interfaces, and gives the organization visibility and control it otherwise lacks. It performs discovery, revealing which cloud services are actually in use across the organization, which routinely surprises leadership with its breadth. It enforces policy on cloud use, governing who may use which services and what they may do within them, blocking risky services and constraining sanctioned ones. It extends data protection into the cloud, applying data-loss-prevention controls to information moving into and within cloud applications, and it can enforce encryption and access controls on cloud-resident data. It also provides threat protection, detecting compromised accounts and anomalous behavior in cloud services, such as a user suddenly downloading vastly more than usual or logging in from two distant places at once. The CASB exists because data and applications left the perimeter, and someone had to extend governance to where they went; it is the control that follows the data into the cloud.

From perimeter to cloud edge: a migration perspective

It helps to see the modern architecture not as a clean-sheet design but as the destination of a migration that most organizations are somewhere along, because almost no one rebuilds from scratch and the realistic question is how to evolve what already exists. The starting point is the traditional design this book has described as the castle and moat: a corporate network with a hardened perimeter, a data center holding the applications, security appliances at the edge, and remote users hauled back through a VPN to be inspected centrally. That design worked when the applications lived in the data center and the users sat in the office, and it does not fail all at once. It degrades gradually as reality diverges from its assumptions. As applications move to the cloud, routing user traffic back to the data center only to send it out again to the cloud becomes an absurd and slow detour. As the workforce becomes remote, the office perimeter protects an ever-smaller share of activity. As data spreads across cloud services adopted by individual teams, the things worth protecting increasingly sit entirely outside the moat.

The migration toward the architecture of this chapter proceeds by addressing these gaps as they hurt, rather than by a single grand replacement. An organization might first extend identity and multi-factor authentication everywhere and adopt a CASB to regain visibility into the cloud applications already in use, since you cannot govern what you cannot see. It might then introduce zero trust network access for the applications where broad VPN access is most clearly excessive, granting per-application access while the legacy VPN continues to serve the rest. It might adopt a secure web gateway in the cloud so that remote users' web traffic is inspected near them rather than backhauled, and progressively shift more security functions to the cloud edge until the SASE model is substantially realized. Microsegmentation is introduced where the blast radius of a compromise most needs shrinking, often starting with the crown-jewel systems, rather than everywhere at once. The point of describing it as a journey is to set realistic expectations: the modern architecture is assembled over years, in an order driven by where the old model is failing most painfully and where the organization's risk most demands attention, and an organization can capture much of the benefit incrementally without ever having a single day on which it declares itself transformed. What matters is the direction: toward identity as the perimeter, verification replacing implicit trust, security following the user and the data to wherever they have gone, and the steady, prioritized movement in that direction as the old assumptions continue to erode.

Putting the modern architecture in perspective

It is tempting, after a tour through zero trust, microsegmentation, and SASE, to imagine that sophisticated architecture is what keeps an organization safe. Architecture helps enormously, and for organizations whose work has genuinely moved to the cloud and the home office, it is increasingly the natural fit rather than an aspiration. But we cannot forget the fundamentals, because the basics are what matter most. A beautifully segmented, zero-trust, cloud-delivered network full of unpatched servers, default passwords, over-privileged accounts, and uninspected encrypted traffic is still a breach waiting to happen. Architecture gives you containment, verification, consistent policy, and detection. The fundamentals, including patching, hardening, least privilege, strong authentication, sound firewall policy, and traffic inspection, give you prevention, which means there is less to contain in the first place. Build the modern architecture where it fits, but never let its sophistication distract from the unglamorous basics. Attackers are not impressed by architecture diagrams. They are stopped by patched systems, strong authentication, and someone watching the logs, which is exactly where the next chapters turn.

Chapter 11: DNS and Email Security

IN THIS CHAPTER

- Why these two belong together
- How DNS works
- DNS as an attack surface, and how to defend it
- How email security is built on DNS
- Email security beyond authentication

Why these two belong together

The *Domain Name System (DNS)* and email are treated together here for a reason that surprises newcomers: the modern defenses for email are built almost entirely on DNS records. Understanding how DNS works is therefore a prerequisite for understanding email security, and both are foundational internet services that attackers target precisely because they are everywhere, trusted implicitly, and often poorly defended. Both also predate the hostile internet and were designed in an era of mutual trust, which is why securing them has meant retrofitting authentication and integrity onto protocols that originally assumed everyone was honest.

How DNS works

The *Domain Name System* is the internet's address book. Humans use names like a company's website address; computers route traffic using numeric IP addresses; DNS is the distributed system that translates the former into the latter, billions of times a second, so seamlessly that most people never know it exists until it fails. It is hierarchical and delegated, which is what lets a single naming system serve the entire planet without any central bottleneck.

At the top sit the *root servers*, which know where to find the servers for each *top-level domain*, the suffix at the end of an address. Those in turn point to the *authoritative servers* for individual domains, which hold the actual records that say where a given name lives. When your computer needs to reach a name, it typically asks a *recursive resolver*, which walks this hierarchy on your behalf, asking the root, then the top-level domain, then the authoritative server, and caches the answer so it need not repeat the journey for a while. This delegation and caching is the genius of the design, but each layer is also a place where things can be attacked or quietly go wrong.

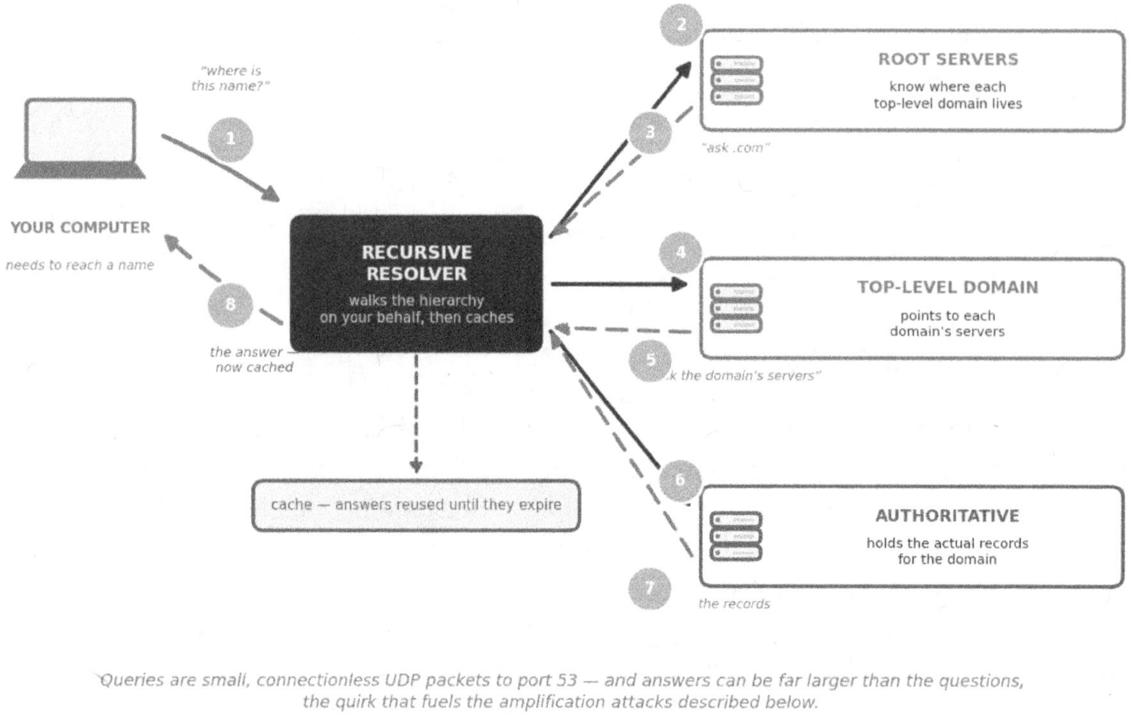

FIGURE 11.1 A recursive DNS query — the resolver walks the hierarchy on your behalf and caches the answer.

A note on the mechanics matters for the attacks below: DNS queries are typically small, connectionless UDP packets sent to port 53, and the responses they elicit can be substantially larger than the queries that prompted them. That quirk becomes important when we discuss amplification attacks.

DNS stores several types of *records*, and a working knowledge of the common ones is part of the job, because reading a domain's records tells you a great deal about how it is configured and what protections it is missing. An *A record* maps a name to an IPv4 address, and an *AAAA record* maps it to an IPv6 address. A *CNAME* is an alias, pointing one name at another so they resolve to the same place. An *MX record* designates the mail servers that receive email for a domain and is central to the email discussion below. *NS records* delegate a domain to its authoritative name servers, and the *SOA record*, or start of authority, holds administrative information about the zone, such as its primary server and how long others should cache its data. A *PTR record* supports reverse lookups, turning an address back into a name, which mail systems use as a sanity check on senders. A *TXT record* holds arbitrary text and has become the workhorse for verification and policy, carrying, among other things, the email-authentication records discussed shortly. A *CAA record* specifies which certificate authorities are permitted to issue certificates for a domain, a useful guard against a rogue or tricked authority issuing a fraudulent certificate. An *SRV record* advertises the location of particular services. Knowing what each record does lets you read a domain's configuration like a sentence and spot immediately what is absent or wrong.

TABLE 11.1 Common DNS record types

Record	What it does
A	Maps a name to an IPv4 address.
AAAA	Maps a name to an IPv6 address.
CNAME	An alias — points one name at another so they resolve to the same place.
MX	Designates the mail servers that receive email for a domain; central to email security.
NS	Delegates a domain to its authoritative name servers.
SOA	Start of authority — administrative information about the zone, such as its primary server and how long others should cache its data.
PTR	Supports reverse lookups, turning an address back into a name; mail systems use it as a sanity check on senders.
TXT	Holds arbitrary text — the workhorse for verification and policy, carrying among other things the email-authentication records.
CAA	Specifies which certificate authorities may issue certificates for a domain — a guard against a rogue or tricked authority.
SRV	Advertises the location of particular services.

Reading a domain's records tells you a great deal about how it is configured and what protections it is missing.

DNS as an attack surface, and how to defend it

Because DNS is so fundamental and because nearly all traffic depends on its answers being correct, it is an attractive target, and attackers abuse it in several distinct ways. In *cache poisoning*, an attacker tricks a resolver into caching a false answer, so that users seeking a legitimate site are silently directed to a malicious one without anything appearing wrong to them. In *DNS hijacking*, an attacker gains control of a domain's records outright, often by compromising the account at the domain registrar or DNS provider rather than by attacking the protocol, and redirects the domain wholesale. This is devastating because controlling a domain's DNS can also let the attacker obtain valid certificates for it and intercept its email.

DNS is also abused as a covert channel. In *DNS tunneling*, data is smuggled into and out of a network encoded inside DNS queries and responses, slipping past controls that wave DNS traffic through without inspection. This technique is used both for data exfiltration and for malware command-and-control because DNS is so rarely blocked. A related and often overlooked failure is *subdomain takeover*, in which a domain has a record, typically a CNAME, pointing at a third-party service such as a cloud storage bucket or a hosting platform, and the organization stops using the service without removing the dangling record. An attacker who notices the abandoned reference can claim the resource on the third-party platform and now controls a subdomain of the victim's domain, useful for phishing, for stealing session cookies that scope to the parent domain, and for any attack that benefits from appearing to come from a trusted brand.

Closely related, though not strictly attacks on DNS itself, are *typosquatting* and *homograph domains*. In these attacks, adversaries register names that look identical or nearly identical to legitimate ones, exploiting either common typing mistakes or visually similar Unicode characters from other alphabets, and then use those domains for phishing or to host malicious content. This technique combines especially dangerously with the email authentication discussed later, since an attacker who registers a lookalike domain can publish valid SPF, DKIM, and DMARC records for it and send phishing mail that is technically authenticated. The system's reliance on fast, connectionless queries also makes it both a tool and a target for denial-of-service attacks, including *amplification attacks* that abuse misconfigured open resolvers to flood a victim with far more traffic than the attacker sent.

The defenses follow the threats. *DNSSEC* adds cryptographic signatures to DNS records so that a resolver can verify an answer genuinely came from the authoritative source and was not altered in transit, addressing the integrity-and-authenticity gap that enables cache poisoning. It does not, however, provide confidentiality; it proves the answer is genuine, not that nobody saw the query, a distinction worth keeping straight. Confidentiality of DNS queries is addressed separately by *DNS over HTTPS* and *DNS over TLS*, which encrypt the queries themselves so that an eavesdropper on the network cannot see, or tamper with, which names a user is looking up. These improve privacy but, notably, also complicate an organization's own visibility into DNS, an example of the recurring tension between privacy and inspection that ran through the decryption chapter.

Protective DNS, also called *DNS filtering*, turns the system into a security control in its own right. By using a resolver that refuses to resolve known-malicious domains, an organization can block a great deal of malware, phishing, and command-and-control cheaply and at a single chokepoint, since so many attacks depend on resolving a name at some stage. This complements the URL filtering of the firewall, with the two operating as parallel chokepoints so that an attack must evade both name resolution and connection inspection. Finally, because DNS hijacking so often begins at the registrar rather than in the protocol, protecting the registrar and DNS-provider accounts with strong, phishing-resistant authentication, and locking domains against unauthorized transfer, is a high-value and frequently neglected control that has nothing to do with DNS technology and everything to do with the account security of the identity chapter.

How email security is built on DNS

Email was designed in a more trusting era, with no built-in way to verify that a message claiming to come from a domain actually did. This omission is the root of spam, phishing, and the spoofing that lets an attacker forge a message appearing to come from your own organization or a trusted partner. Given that phishing is the single most common way attackers gain their initial foothold, closing this gap is among the highest-value work in all of security. The fix was a layered set of authentication mechanisms, and crucially, they are published as DNS records on the sending domain, which is why DNS and email share this chapter. Three mechanisms form the core, and they build on one another in a deliberate sequence.

SPF, the Sender Policy Framework, lets a domain publish, in a DNS TXT record, the list of mail servers authorized to send email on its behalf. A receiving server can then check whether a message arrived from an authorized source and treat it with suspicion if not. SPF authenticates the path the mail took, meaning which server sent it, rather than the message itself, and it has well-known limits. It breaks when mail is forwarded, because the forwarding server is not on the original sender's authorized list, and the standard permits only a limited number of DNS lookups in evaluating a policy, which sprawling configurations can exceed and thereby fail. The policy ends with an instruction about what to do with mail from unauthorized sources, ranging from a soft suggestion to treat it with suspicion to a hard demand to reject it.

DKIM, DomainKeys Identified Mail, addresses what SPF cannot: it cryptographically signs the message itself. The sending server signs outgoing mail with a private key, and the corresponding public key is published, again in DNS, so that the receiver can verify the signature, confirming both that the message genuinely came from the claimed domain and that it was not altered in transit. Because the signature travels with the message, DKIM survives forwarding in a way SPF does not, which is one reason both are used together rather than either alone. The public key lives at a location identified by a *selector*, a label that lets a domain publish several keys for different mail streams and rotate them over time without disruption, the same key-lifecycle hygiene the encryption chapter urged for keys generally.

DMARC, Domain-based Message Authentication, Reporting and Conformance, ties the first two together and makes them enforceable. Published as a DNS TXT record at a defined location for the domain, a DMARC policy tells receiving servers what to do with mail that fails authentication: do nothing, quarantine it to the spam folder, or reject it outright. It also adds the essential concept of *alignment*, requiring that the domain validated by SPF or DKIM actually matches the domain the user sees in the visible "from" line, which closes spoofing tricks that SPF and DKIM alone permit by authenticating a domain other than the one the recipient reads. Just as valuable, DMARC provides reporting. Receivers send back aggregate reports about mail claiming to be from your domain, giving you visibility into who is sending as you, legitimate and fraudulent alike. This is often the first time an organization discovers both forgotten legitimate mail streams and active impersonation. The standard discipline is to deploy DMARC first in its do-nothing, report-only mode to learn what your real mail looks like without disrupting anything, then tighten progressively to quarantine and finally to reject as confidence grows. Moving straight to reject can silently block legitimate mail you did not know existed, turning a security improvement into a self-inflicted outage.

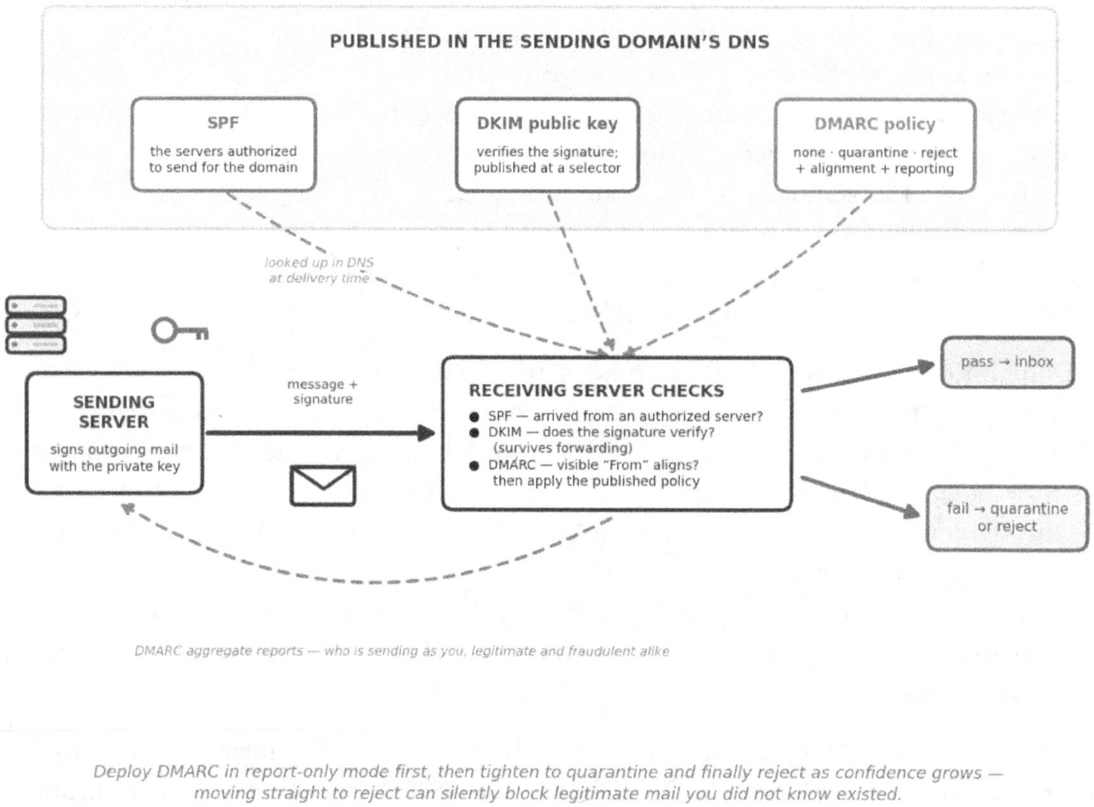

FIGURE 11.2 Email authentication — SPF, DKIM, and DMARC published in DNS and checked at delivery.

TABLE 11.2 The three email-authentication mechanisms

Mechanism	What it authenticates	Known limits
SPF	The path the mail took — publishes in a DNS TXT record the servers authorized to send for the domain	Breaks when mail is forwarded; a limited number of DNS lookups that sprawling configurations can exceed
DKIM	The message itself — the sending server signs outgoing mail; the public key is published in DNS at a selector	Survives forwarding in a way SPF does not, which is why both are used together
DMARC	Ties the first two together — requires alignment with the visible "from" and tells receivers what to do on failure: none, quarantine, or reject	Deploy in report-only mode first; moving straight to reject can silently block legitimate mail

Several further records extend this foundation, and a thorough mail configuration uses them. *BIMI*, Brand Indicators for Message Identification, lets a domain that enforces DMARC display its verified logo beside its messages in supporting mail clients, both as a trust signal to recipients and as an incentive to reach full enforcement. It generally requires a verified mark certificate proving the organization owns the logo. *MTA-STS* lets a domain require that incoming mail be delivered over encrypted, authenticated connections, closing a historical gap in which mail transport encryption was optional and could be silently downgraded by an attacker. Its companion, *TLS-RPT*, provides reporting on transport-encryption failures so you can detect both problems and attacks against mail delivery. *DANE*, which builds on DNSSEC, offers another route to binding mail-server certificates to the domain so that encryption cannot be stripped. *ARC*, Authenticated Received Chain, preserves authentication results across intermediaries such as mailing lists and forwarders, mitigating the forwarding problem that bedevils SPF.

You will not need every one of these for every domain, but knowing the toolkit lets you assemble the right combination. At minimum, every domain that sends mail should publish SPF, DKIM, and an enforced DMARC policy. Their absence is among the most common and most exploited gaps on the internet, and closing it is one of the highest-value, lowest-cost improvements available to any organization.

Email security beyond authentication

Authentication records stop spoofing, but they do not stop a genuine phishing message sent from an attacker's own authenticated domain, so email defense needs more. *Secure email gateways* filter inbound mail for spam, malware, and phishing, scanning attachments, often by detonating them in a sandbox, as the malware chapter describes, and rewriting or checking links so that a message whose link was benign at delivery is re-checked when the user actually clicks. Because attackers increasingly use links to credential-harvesting pages rather than malicious attachments, this click-time protection matters.

None of it is complete, which returns us to the human layer. The technical controls blunt the volume and catch the obvious, but the well-crafted message aimed at a specific person will sometimes arrive, which is why the non-punitive training and rapid reporting culture urged in the threats chapter remains the irreplaceable last layer. The combination of authentication records to stop spoofing, gateways to filter the bulk, and trained people to catch and report the rest is what a serious email-security posture looks like, and the absence of any one layer leaves a gap the others cannot fully cover.

Chapter 12: Security Operations — Logging, Monitoring, SIEM, and SOAR

IN THIS CHAPTER

Operations is where security actually happens

Everything built in the preceding chapters, including the firewalls, the identity systems, the segmented architecture, and the encryption, is potential security. It becomes actual security only when someone operates it: watches it, tends it, notices when it fails, and acts. *Security operations* is that ongoing work, and it is where most real defending happens, far from the architecture diagrams and the procurement decisions. This chapter and the next two cover the operational disciplines: monitoring and the orchestration that scales it, the management of vulnerabilities and changes, and the response when something goes wrong. They share a common theme: security is sustained, not achieved. They also share a common enemy, which is the gap between what an organization believes it is doing and what it is actually doing.

Logging: the raw material of everything

Operations rests on *logging*, the records that systems generate about what is happening: who logged in and from where, what changed, what was accessed, what was blocked, what errored, and what an application did. Logs are the raw material of detection, investigation, and response, and the first practical task is ensuring that the right things are logged in the first place. A log that was never generated cannot be reviewed after the fact, and many organizations discover during an incident, at the worst possible moment, that the evidence they desperately need was never being recorded. Deciding what to log is itself a skill: log too little and you are blind; log everything indiscriminately and you drown in volume and cost while the signal hides in the noise. The firewalls of the earlier chapters are prolific and valuable log sources, recording what traffic was allowed and denied, what applications and users were seen, what threats were blocked, and what was decrypted. So are identity systems, endpoints, servers, applications, and cloud services. A useful principle is to log what you would need to answer the questions an investigation will ask: who did what, when, from where, and to what effect. Those logs should capture enough context to be meaningful rather than becoming a stream of cryptic codes.

Logs are only useful if they are trustworthy and available, which raises two operational requirements. First, *centralization*: logs scattered across hundreds of individual systems are nearly useless for detection, because no human can watch them all, and an attacker who compromises a system can tamper with or delete its local logs to cover their tracks. Collecting logs into a central, protected repository solves both problems at once. It enables analysis across systems, and it preserves the evidence beyond the reach of an attacker who has compromised the source, since the record was copied away before they could erase it. Second, *retention and integrity*: logs must be kept long enough to be useful, which is often longer than intuition suggests because breaches are frequently discovered months after they begin. The logs must also be protected against alteration so they can be trusted in an investigation or, if it comes to it, in court. Regulatory regimes frequently dictate minimum retention periods, tying this operational detail back to the compliance chapter.

Monitoring and the SIEM

Collecting logs is necessary but not sufficient; someone or something must watch them, which is the work of *monitoring*. The tool at the center of this is typically a *security information and event management system (SIEM)*, which aggregates logs from across the environment and, crucially, correlates them, connecting events that are individually unremarkable but together tell a story. A single failed login is noise. Failed logins against many accounts from one source, followed by a success, followed by that account suddenly reaching systems it never normally touches and transferring data outward, is the unmistakable signature of an attack in progress, and correlation is what assembles that narrative from the flood of disconnected events. The SIEM is the place where the signals from firewalls, identity systems, intrusion detection, endpoints, DNS, and cloud services converge, turning a scatter of separate alarms into a coherent picture of what is happening across the whole environment. This is exactly the visibility an attacker hopes you lack.

The honest caveat, repeated because it is so often ignored, is that a SIEM is a powerful tool and a demanding one. Poorly tuned, it floods analysts with *false positives*, alerts that look like attacks but turn out to be normal activity, and the sheer volume produces the well-documented problem of *alert fatigue*, in which analysts faced with thousands of daily alerts begin, quite rationally, to ignore them. The danger is that the one real alert hides among the false ones, unnoticed until the damage is done. A SIEM is not a product you buy and switch on; it is a capability you tune continuously, deciding what matters, suppressing what does not, writing and refining the correlation rules that turn raw logs into meaningful detections, and adjusting as the environment and the threats change. Recommending a SIEM without also recommending the training and skilled staff needed to set it up, monitor it, and continuously refine it is setting up an expensive disappointment.

Unfortunately, many organizations end up with a SIEM that technically functions while detecting nothing useful. The reasons vary: sometimes the tool was bought primarily to check a monitoring requirement off an audit or compliance checklist, sometimes the organization lacked the experience to know what operating a SIEM actually required, and sometimes the budget covered the purchase but not the skilled staff, time, and ongoing effort needed to make it work. The outcome is the same: it turns into what is sometimes called *shelfware*, software that sits on the shelf and is never really used. It is a pattern that recurs throughout this book whenever security tools are bought as artifacts rather than operated as capabilities.

Detecting anomalies depends on a sense of *baseline*: knowing what normal looks like in this environment, which systems talk to which, at what volumes and at what hours, so that deviations announce themselves. Without a baseline, everything looks equally plausible and nothing stands out. With one, the server that suddenly sends large volumes of data to an unfamiliar destination, the account active at an hour its owner is asleep, and the workstation reaching for systems it has no business touching all become visible as the anomalies they are.

Reporting and the human function of operations

Beyond detection, operations produces *reporting*, and its purpose is often misunderstood as bureaucratic when it is in fact how security communicates with the rest of the organization and improves itself. Operational reporting serves several distinct audiences and ends. *Compliance reporting* demonstrates to auditors and regulators that controls are operating as required, drawing directly on the logs and monitoring described above. *Management reporting* translates the technical reality into terms leadership can act on: the trends in attacks seen and blocked, the state of patching and vulnerabilities, the incidents handled, and the lessons learned. This allows the people who allocate budget and accept risk to do so with a true picture rather than a hopeful one. *Operational metrics* track how well the function itself is performing, such as how quickly threats are detected and how quickly they are responded to, because the time between an attacker's entry and their detection is one of the most consequential numbers in all of security, and managing it requires measuring it. The discipline of reporting also forces a regular, honest look at the environment that surfaces the slow drift: the growing pile of unpatched systems, the creeping increase in alerts ignored, and the weaknesses that no single day's work would reveal. Reporting, done well, is not paperwork; it is the feedback loop by which a security program sees itself clearly and gets better.

Threat hunting and knowing your log sources

Monitoring as described so far is largely reactive: the systems watch for known patterns and anomalies and raise alerts when something matches. A more advanced operational discipline, *threat hunting*, is deliberately proactive. Skilled analysts form hypotheses about how an attacker might be operating undetected in the environment and go looking for evidence of it, rather than waiting for an alert. The premise of threat hunting is the *assume-breach mindset* taken seriously: if you accept that an attacker may already be inside and evading your automated detection, then someone should be actively hunting for them rather than trusting that the alerts would have fired. A hunt might begin with a hypothesis drawn from knowledge of attacker techniques: "if an adversary were establishing persistence this way, we would see this trace in these logs." The analyst then queries the centralized data to confirm or refute it, turning up either an intrusion that automated detection missed or, valuably, a gap in detection that can then be closed by writing a new rule. Threat hunting both finds the attacks that slip past automation and continuously improves the automation, and it depends entirely on having good, centralized, retained log data to hunt through, which is why the logging discipline earlier in this chapter is its prerequisite.

Hunting and detection alike depend on understanding what each *log source* can tell you, because different sources illuminate different parts of an attack and the picture is only complete when they are correlated. Firewall and network logs reveal connections, scanning, lateral movement between systems, and command-and-control traffic reaching outward, providing the network view of an attack in progress. Identity and authentication logs reveal logins, failures, privilege use, and the account compromise and escalation that underpin most intrusions, often the earliest sign that credentials have been stolen. Endpoint logs and the recordings of endpoint detection tools reveal what actually happened on a machine: the processes that ran, the files that changed, and the persistence that was established. This is the ground truth that network logs can only infer. DNS logs reveal the names systems looked up, exposing both the command-and-control domains malware contacts and the tunneling that hides data in DNS queries. Cloud and application logs reveal activity in the services where data increasingly lives. The art of detection is knowing that an attack leaves different footprints in each of these, that any single source tells only part of the story, and that correlation across them, the central function of the SIEM, is what assembles the fragments into the recognizable shape of an intrusion. A defender who understands their log sources knows where to look for each kind of attacker behavior; one who does not is searching in the dark even with all the data in hand.

SOAR: orchestration and automation

A SIEM that detects more than its analysts can handle has only relocated the bottleneck, and as the volume and speed of attacks have grown, the answer has been to automate the response. This is the role of *security orchestration, automation, and response (SOAR)*. Where the SIEM detects and correlates, SOAR acts: it connects the many tools of a security environment together and runs predefined workflows, called *playbooks*, that carry out the repetitive, well-understood parts of response automatically and at machine speed. When the SIEM detects a likely compromise, a SOAR playbook might automatically gather relevant context from across the environment, pulling the logs, checking the reputation of the addresses involved, querying the identity system about the user, and presenting the analyst with an assembled case rather than a bare alert. For high-confidence detections, it may take containing action directly, such as isolating an affected endpoint, disabling a compromised account, or blocking a malicious address at the firewall, all in the seconds it would take a human merely to read the alert.

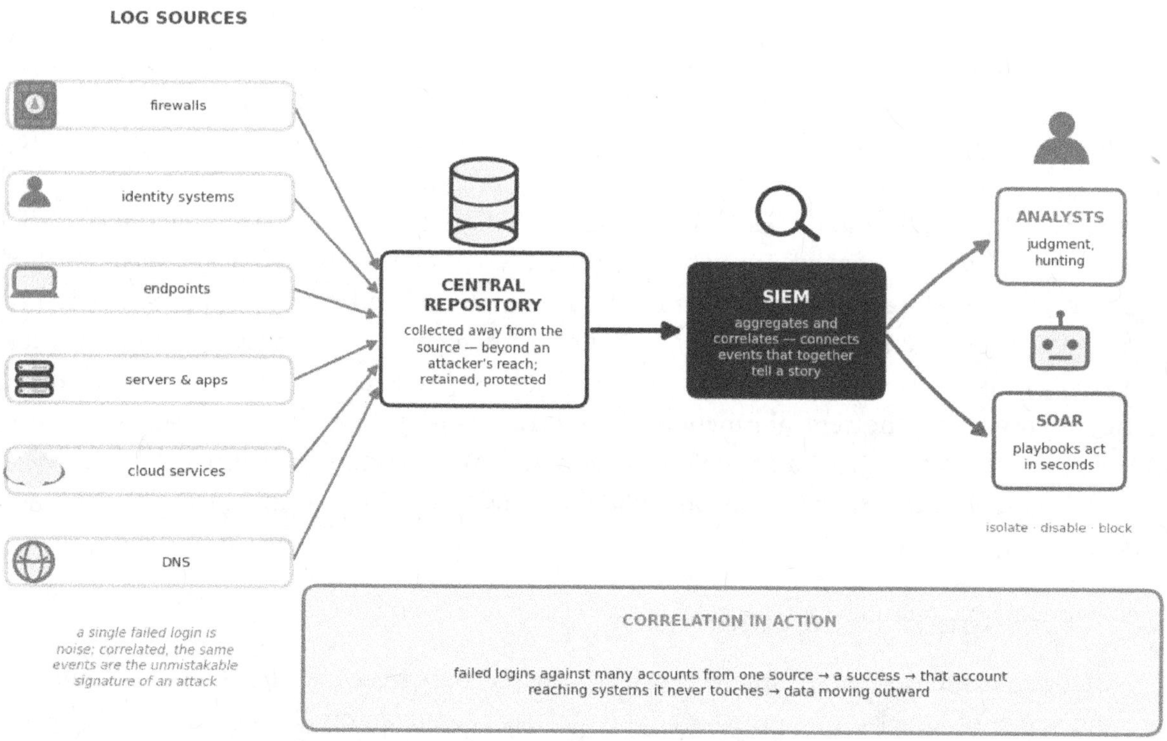

FIGURE 12.1 The operations pipeline — logs centralized, correlated by the SIEM, acted on by analysts and SOAR playbooks.

The value of SOAR is twofold and worth stating plainly. It speeds response, compressing the time between detection and action from the minutes or hours a human takes to the seconds a machine takes, which directly shrinks the window in which an attacker operates. Since attackers increasingly move fast and automate their own work, defenders who respond at human speed alone are losing a race. SOAR also frees skilled people from the grinding repetition of routine triage to focus on the judgment-intensive work that automation cannot do: the genuinely novel incident, the ambiguous case, and the investigation that requires intuition and experience. The honest limits matter too: automation does exactly what its playbooks tell it, so a poorly designed playbook can take a wrong action quickly and at scale. This is why automated containment is usually reserved for high-confidence cases and why playbooks are built carefully and tested like any other critical system. Used well, the combination of SIEM and SOAR—detection at scale feeding response at speed—is what lets a security operations function defend a large, fast-moving environment that no amount of human effort alone could watch. It does not replace the analyst; it makes the analyst's attention go where it is actually needed, which, given how scarce skilled security people are, may be the most important thing operations can do.

Chapter 13: Vulnerability Management and the Secure Deployment Lifecycle

IN THIS CHAPTER

The unglamorous control that prevents the most harm
Vulnerability management as the larger discipline
Penetration testing and red teaming
Security in the deployment lifecycle: shift left
Change management: deploying with control

The unglamorous control that prevents the most harm

If asked to name the single most important operational practice in security, many seasoned professionals would say *patching*, keeping software up to date so that known vulnerabilities are fixed before attackers exploit them. It is unglamorous, endless, and easy to deprioritize, and it prevents an enormous share of real-world breaches, because attackers overwhelmingly exploit known vulnerabilities for which a patch already exists rather than expensive unknown ones. The economics drive this: a known vulnerability with a published patch is cheap to exploit, since the patch itself reveals the flaw and the unpatched systems are plentiful, while an unknown vulnerability is expensive to discover and precious to the attacker who holds it. Every major breach traced back to a months-old unpatched flaw, and there have been many famous ones, is a failure of this discipline, not a triumph of attacker ingenuity.

The reason patching is hard is not that anyone disputes its importance but that doing it well, at scale, without breaking things, is genuinely difficult. Patches occasionally cause problems of their own, breaking the very systems they were meant to protect. Systems cannot always be taken offline at will, especially those that run continuously or that the business depends on minute to minute. Some software is too old to patch, or runs on systems that cannot be touched without unacceptable risk. And new vulnerabilities are disclosed every single day, so the work is never finished. Treating patching as a project to complete rather than a process to sustain is a common and costly mistake, and the organizations that do it well treat it as routine infrastructure, like keeping the lights on, rather than as a series of emergencies.

Vulnerability management as the larger discipline

Patching is one part of a broader practice called *vulnerability management*: the ongoing cycle of finding the weaknesses in an environment, judging which ones matter most, fixing or mitigating them, and verifying that the fix worked. It begins with *discovery*, typically through *vulnerability scanning*, automated tools that probe systems for known weaknesses and produce, almost always, far more findings than anyone could ever address at once. The first scan of a neglected environment can return tens of thousands of findings, and the natural reaction of despair is precisely the wrong one.

This is where the risk thinking of the early chapters becomes indispensable, because the central challenge of vulnerability management is not finding vulnerabilities. The scanner does that. The central challenge is *prioritizing* them. You will never patch everything immediately, so you must decide what to fix first, and the naive approach that simply sorts by a published severity score is badly incomplete. A sophisticated prioritization weighs that severity against context: Is this vulnerability on an internet-facing system an attacker can actually reach, or buried deep inside a segmented network behind several other controls? Is it being actively exploited in the wild right now, which transforms a theoretical risk into an urgent one, or is it merely theoretically exploitable? Does it sit on a system holding the organization's most sensitive data or running its most critical service, or on something trivial? A medium-severity flaw on an exposed, critical, actively exploited system deserves attention long before a high-severity flaw on an isolated system that no threat can reach. Prioritizing by real, contextual risk rather than by raw score is exactly what separates effective vulnerability management from drowning in a scanner's output, and it is the single most valuable judgment in the whole discipline.

A sustainable practice has a few recognizable features. It maintains the inventory of the assets chapter, because you cannot patch what you do not know exists, and the unknown system is both the one that goes unpatched and the one the scanner may not even reach. It establishes a regular cadence for routine patches and a faster emergency track for the critical, actively exploited vulnerabilities that cannot wait for the normal cycle. It tests significant patches before broad deployment where feasible, often by rolling out to a small set of systems first, to catch the patches that break things before they break everything. This balances the risk of the patch against the risk of the vulnerability it fixes, which is itself a risk decision. It accepts that some systems cannot be patched promptly and wraps those in *compensating controls*, such as extra segmentation, tighter monitoring, and restricted access, to reduce the risk that cannot be eliminated. This is how the unpatchable legacy system is managed rather than merely feared. And it verifies, rather than assumes, that patches actually applied, closing the loop between intention and reality, because the gap between "we have a patching policy" and "every system is actually patched" is exactly where breaches live.

Penetration testing and red teaming

Scanning finds known vulnerabilities, but it does not tell you whether they can actually be chained into a real attack, nor does it find the weaknesses that come from how systems are combined rather than from any single flaw. For that, organizations turn to active testing by skilled humans. *Penetration testing* has testers attempt to compromise systems as a real attacker would, within an agreed scope, surfacing weaknesses that automated scans miss and, crucially, revealing how individual flaws chain together into a genuine attack path, since real breaches usually string several small weaknesses into one serious one. *Red teaming* goes broader, simulating a realistic adversary against the whole organization, including its people and processes and its ability to detect and respond, to test not just whether a system can be breached but whether the defenders would notice and react. These exercises are valuable precisely because they test reality rather than configuration, and a finding from a competent penetration test, such as "here is exactly how we got from the internet to your customer database," is far more persuasive to leadership than any abstract risk assessment. The honest caveat is that their value depends entirely on the skill of the testers and the honesty of the scope, and that a test treated as a checkbox, scoped so narrowly that it cannot fail, teaches nothing.

Security in the deployment lifecycle: shift left

A recurring, expensive pattern in immature organizations is to design and build something, deploy it, and only then ask the security team to "secure it." This is backward and far more costly than doing it right, because security retrofitted onto a finished system is always more expensive, less effective, and more disruptive than security designed in from the start. The professional principle is to involve security from the planning stage of any hardware or software deployment, so that security requirements shape the design rather than fighting it afterward. This approach is often called *shifting left*, moving security earlier in the lifecycle toward the beginning. The justification is simple economics of defect cost: a flawed design caught on a whiteboard costs a conversation, the same flaw caught after deployment costs a re-architecture, and the same flaw caught after a breach costs far more than money. The earlier a problem is found, the cheaper it is to fix, and security's most valuable contribution to any project is often the shaping question asked early: what data will this handle, who needs access, what is it exposed to, how will we update it, and how will we know if it is attacked? At that stage, the answers can still influence the design at the cost of a discussion rather than a rebuild.

Planning is where you establish what "secure enough" means for this particular system, using the risk analysis of the early chapters. You determine what the system will handle and therefore how sensitive it is, what it must be protected against given your threat assumptions, and what controls the design must include as a result. You consider how it will fit into the existing architecture: which segment or zone it belongs in, what it needs to communicate with, how access will be controlled, and whether its traffic will be inspected. And you plan for the whole lifecycle, not just the launch: how the system will be monitored, how it will be patched and updated, and eventually how it will be retired and its data securely disposed of, because systems that cannot be maintained or safely decommissioned become tomorrow's forgotten liabilities. Planning for the end of life at the beginning sounds excessive until you have inherited a critical system that nobody knows how to update or dares to turn off.

Before a new system or significant change goes into production, it should be tested, and security testing is a distinct and necessary part of that rather than an afterthought folded into functional testing. *Functional testing* and *integration testing* confirm the thing works and works with its neighbors, which has security relevance because failures and unexpected interactions are often where vulnerabilities hide. Vulnerability scanning checks the new system for known weaknesses before it is exposed rather than after. Penetration testing, where warranted, has skilled testers actively attempt to compromise it. And *configuration review* checks the system against hardening baselines to confirm it was actually built securely rather than merely intended to be. A practice worth insisting on is a separate *testing environment* that mirrors production, so that testing, patch deployment, and changes can happen without risking the live systems and the data they hold. Testing security changes directly in production is how organizations cause the very outages they were trying to prevent.

Change management: deploying with control

When a tested system or change is finally deployed, the deployment itself should be controlled rather than improvised, through the practice of *change management*: reviewing, approving, documenting, and scheduling changes. The reasons become obvious the first time an unreviewed change causes an outage or quietly opens a hole. Change management ensures that changes are reviewed by someone other than the person making them, but more than that, it structures communication across the different groups and stakeholders who may be affected. It draws in subject matter experts and diverse perspectives that the person making the change may lack, and it enforces *separation of duties* through formal approval gates so that no single person can unilaterally move a change from proposal to production. This catches mistakes and bad ideas before they ship, but it also surfaces operational, security, and business concerns that only emerge when the right people are in the room.

Additionally, change management maintains a record of not just what changed and when, but why: the approval, reasoning, context, and alternatives considered behind each decision. This *decision provenance* is what separates a change log from institutional knowledge. It allows future engineers to understand not only the state of the system but the thinking that shaped it, preventing the costly and dangerous pattern of relitigating settled decisions or unknowingly reversing them. That record is invaluable for troubleshooting, since the recent-changes list is the first place to look when something breaks, and for the incident investigation of the next chapter, since an attacker's actions often hide among or masquerade as legitimate changes. It also preserves the ability to *roll back*, to undo a change that turns out badly, which transforms a deployment from a leap of faith into a reversible step.

Over time, a well-maintained change record becomes a form of *institutional knowledge*: a systematic history of how the system evolved, why it looks the way it does, and what was tried and abandoned, protecting against the entropy of staff turnover, faded recollection, and undocumented tribal knowledge. The thread connecting planning, testing, and controlled deployment is that each stage is an opportunity to catch problems while they are still cheap, which is defense in depth applied to time rather than to architecture: multiple stages, each catching what the others miss, so that a problem must survive planning review, testing, and change review to reach production, and most do not.

Chapter 14: Incident Response and Malware Analysis

IN THIS CHAPTER

- Assume you will be breached
- The phases of incident response
- Building readiness: tabletop exercises and the value of practice
- Special considerations: breaches, intrusions, and theft
- Malware analysis: understanding what you are fighting

Assume you will be breached

Every honest treatment of security arrives at the same conclusion: you will, at some point, have an incident. The reasoning is unavoidable: prevention is imperfect, attackers are persistent, people make mistakes, and the asymmetry favors the attacker who needs to succeed only once while the defender must succeed always. Maturity, then, is not measured by the absence of incidents, which is unattainable for any interesting target, but by how well you handle the ones that occur. An organization that detects a breach quickly, contains it, recovers, and learns from it has succeeded even though it was breached; one that is breached, fails to notice for months, responds in chaos, and learns nothing has failed even if it was breached only once. This reframing is liberating and clarifying: it directs energy toward detection, response, and recovery rather than toward the impossible fantasy of perfect prevention, and it makes the incident-response capability a core investment rather than an admission of defeat.

This is why *incident response* is a planned capability, not an improvisation. The middle of a breach, with systems compromised, data possibly leaving, executives demanding answers, lawyers asking about notification deadlines, and the clock running, is the worst possible time to figure out who does what. The plan and the practice must exist beforehand, so that when the moment comes, people execute a rehearsed response rather than panic. The difference between an organization that has practiced and one that has only written a plan is stark and immediate the first time a real incident hits.

The phases of incident response

Incident response is conventionally organized into phases, and while different frameworks name them slightly differently, the substance is consistent and worth internalizing as a mental sequence you can run under pressure.

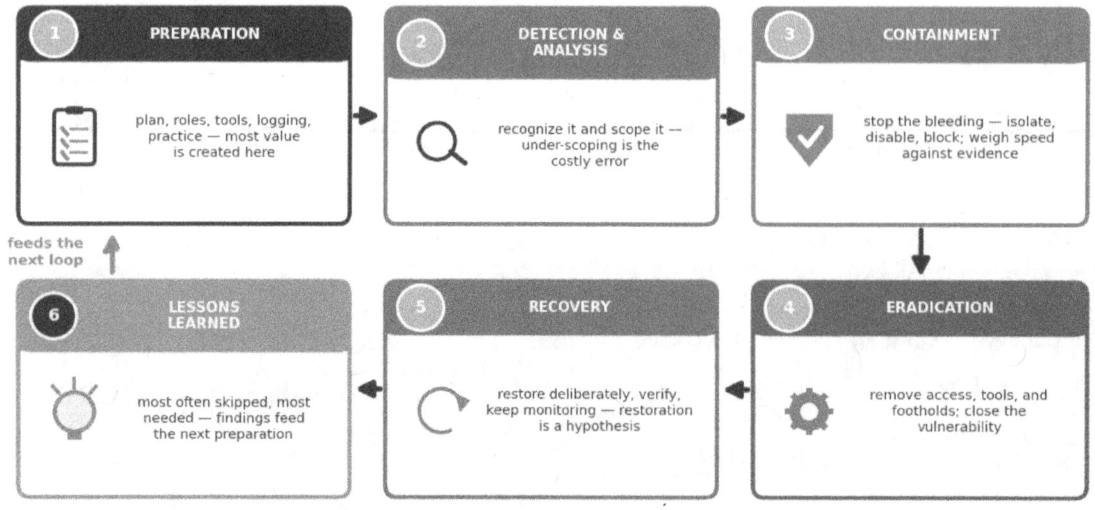

Different frameworks name the phases slightly differently, but the substance is consistent — a mental sequence you can run under pressure.

FIGURE 14.1 The incident-response lifecycle — six phases, with lessons learned feeding the next preparation.

Preparation comes before any incident and is where most of the value is created. It means having a plan that names roles and responsibilities, having the tools and access ready, having the logging and monitoring of the operations chapter in place so that the evidence exists when you need it, and, critically, having practiced. A plan that has never been exercised tends to fall apart on first contact with a real incident. *Tabletop exercises* and drills are what turn a document into a capability.

Among the most consequential failures in incident response, and among the most common, are not technical ones but communication ones: the right people notified too late, escalation paths that stall or skip critical stakeholders, or messaging that gets ahead of the facts. Preparation therefore means establishing communication and escalation paths before they are needed. The organization should know in advance whom to contact and in what order, how to reach them when normal channels are unavailable, and at what thresholds a situation moves up the chain. Those contacts span legal, management, communications, law enforcement, insurers, and any external responders retained on retainer. The point is to avoid searching for phone numbers while the breach unfolds, to engage communications early enough to manage internal and external messaging before it manages itself, and to engage legal early enough to advise on the notification obligations that, as the compliance chapter described, may be running on a strict clock from the moment of discovery.

Detection and analysis is recognizing that an incident is happening and understanding it, drawing on the monitoring, anomaly detection, and correlation of the operations chapter. The goal is to determine what is actually going on: what systems are affected, what the attacker is doing, how they got in, and how serious it is. Misjudging the scope early, by assuming an incident is smaller than it is, is a common and costly error because it leads to under-response and to missed footholds that let the attacker return after you believe you have evicted them.

Containment is stopping the bleeding, limiting the damage before it spreads further. This might mean isolating affected systems entirely or quarantining them in a segmented environment where they remain observable, disabling compromised accounts, or blocking malicious traffic at the firewall, often executed automatically through the SOAR playbooks of the operations chapter. Containment involves a genuine tension worth understanding: act too slowly and the damage grows, but act too hastily and you may tip off the attacker, who can then do destructive damage on the way out, or you may destroy the very evidence you need to understand what happened. There is also a balance between short-term containment that stops immediate harm and longer-term containment that holds the line while you prepare to remove the threat fully.

Eradication is removing the threat entirely: eliminating the attacker's access, removing their tools and footholds, and closing the vulnerability they exploited so they cannot simply walk back in. This requires understanding the full scope, because eradicating what you can see while missing a hidden foothold means the attacker quietly returns, sometimes more carefully and more destructively than before, having learned that you are hunting them.

Recovery is restoring normal operations, bringing systems back to production-level states, restoring data from the backups you maintained and tested, and confirming that everything is clean and functioning before returning it to service. Recovery should be deliberate and verified rather than rushed, because restoring a system that is still compromised, or restoring from a backup that was made after the attacker was already inside, simply reopens the wound and squanders the eradication effort. Verification does not end at the moment of restoration. Continuous monitoring in the period immediately following recovery is essential to confirm that the threat has not persisted, reestablished a foothold, or returned through a vector that eradication missed. A system returned to production is a hypothesis that the threat is gone; monitoring is how you test it.

Lessons learned is the phase organizations most often skip and most need. Once the incident is resolved, the response team steps back to examine what happened, where the response was successful, and where it fell short. The purpose is explicitly not to assign blame, because a blame-driven review teaches people to hide problems, which is precisely the opposite of what you want. The purpose is to ensure that the painful lesson the incident taught is actually learned, so the same gap is not exploited twice. That requires an honest accounting of every bottleneck and breakdown the incident exposed, and those are rarely confined to only technical vulnerabilities. Incidents have a way of surfacing failures of communication, escalation, planning, and preparation that normal operations never would, revealing the organizational fault lines that only become visible under pressure. This is also where the cycle returns to preparation: plans, playbooks, contact lists, and escalation paths are updated to reflect what the incident revealed, turning hard experience into institutional knowledge that strengthens the next response before it begins. The incident that makes an organization measurably stronger has, in a real sense, paid for itself. Done well, lessons learned closes the loop: the end of one incident becomes the starting point for a stronger response to the next.

Building readiness: tabletop exercises and the value of practice

The single largest difference between organizations that handle incidents well and those that handle them badly is rarely the quality of their written plan; it is whether they have practiced. A plan that has only been written and filed tends to reveal its gaps at the worst possible moment, when an actual breach is underway and there is no time to discover that a key contact has left, that no one is sure who has authority to disconnect a critical system, or that the backups everyone assumed were good have never been test-restored. Practice surfaces these gaps in advance, when discovering them is merely instructive rather than catastrophic, which is why mature programs exercise their incident response regularly rather than treating the plan as a document to be admired.

The most common and accessible form of practice is the *tabletop exercise*, a discussion-based walkthrough in which the people who would respond to an incident gather and talk through a realistic scenario: "ransomware has been detected on a critical server; what do we do, who does it, and in what order?" This surfaces confusion, missing information, and unclear authority without touching any real systems. Tabletops are inexpensive and reveal an enormous amount. They expose the decisions no one had thought about, the dependencies no one had documented, and the assumptions that turn out to be wrong. They also build the shared understanding that lets a team move quickly and coherently under pressure rather than arguing about roles while the clock runs. More elaborate exercises range up to full simulations and the red-team engagements of the vulnerability chapter, which test not only the plan but the organization's actual ability to detect and respond to a realistic adversary. They answer the question that matters most, which is not "could we be breached?" but "would we notice, and would we respond well?"

The exercises also feed the lessons-learned discipline forward in time. Just as a real incident should yield improvements, so should a simulated one, and an exercise that surfaces a gap has done its job precisely by finding the weakness before an attacker did. Practice extends beyond the response team, too. Senior leadership should understand their role in a serious incident, including the decisions about disclosure, whether to pay a ransom, and public communication, before they must make those decisions in the glare of a real crisis. An executive thinking through these questions for the first time during an actual breach is an executive likely to decide badly. Readiness, in the end, is not the plan; it is the practiced capability the plan describes. The organizations that invest in practice are the ones that, when the inevitable incident comes, respond with the calm competence of a team that has been here before, if only in rehearsal.

Special considerations: breaches, intrusions, and theft

Different kinds of incidents carry their own considerations beyond the general phases. A *data breach*, in which sensitive information is exposed or stolen, often triggers the legal and regulatory notification obligations of the compliance chapter, with defined timeframes and required disclosures. This is why legal and management must be involved from the first hour and why understanding precisely what data was affected is so important. An *active intrusion*, in which an attacker still has access, calls for particular care around evidence and timing, since premature visible action can cause the attacker to dig in deeper or lash out, while watching too long lets harm accumulate. Theft, whether of data, of devices, or through fraud, intersects with law enforcement. In the case of lost or stolen devices, it is exactly where the encryption-at-rest of the encryption chapter proves its worth: a stolen encrypted laptop is a lost asset, while a stolen unencrypted one is a data breach with all the obligations and costs that entails. Throughout any incident, how you handle evidence matters, both for understanding what happened and for any legal or law-enforcement involvement that follows. Acting in ways that preserve rather than destroy evidence, and keeping careful records of what you do and when, keeps your options open, because you rarely know at the outset whether an incident will end in a quiet internal fix or in litigation and prosecution.

Malware analysis: understanding what you are fighting

When an incident involves malware, as so many do, someone must understand what that malware actually does, and the discipline of taking it apart is *malware analysis*, sometimes loosely called *reverse engineering* when it goes deep. The questions it answers are practical and urgent during an incident: What does this thing do? How does it spread? What systems has it touched, and what has it taken? How do we detect every instance of it across the environment, and how do we make sure we have removed it all? Answering these questions turns a frightening unknown into a defined problem, and it produces the *indicators of compromise*: the file fingerprints, the network addresses it contacts, and the changes it makes that let the rest of the organization hunt for and eradicate every copy.

Malware analysis proceeds along two complementary approaches, usually used together. *Static analysis* examines the malware without running it, inspecting the file's structure, the readable strings inside it, the functions it imports, and, at the deepest level, disassembling it to read the actual machine instructions and understand its logic. Static analysis is safe, since the code never executes, and it can reveal capabilities the malware might not show in any single run. But it is slow and is actively frustrated by attackers who *obfuscate* and *pack* their code, deliberately scrambling or compressing it so that its true form is hidden until it runs, specifically to defeat the static analyst.

Dynamic analysis takes the opposite approach, running the malware in a controlled, isolated environment, called a *sandbox*, and observing what it actually does: what files it creates, what changes it makes to the system, what network connections it attempts, and what other code it tries to download. Dynamic analysis cuts straight through obfuscation, because however the code is scrambled on disk, it must reveal its true behavior when it runs. But it sees only the behavior the malware exhibits in that particular run, and sophisticated malware specifically watches for signs that it is being analyzed, detecting the sandbox and behaving innocently when it suspects it is being observed. This hides its real function from the dynamic analyst exactly as packing hides it from the static one. The two approaches are complementary precisely because each defeats the evasion aimed at the other, and a thorough analysis uses static work to map what the malware can do and dynamic work to confirm what it does do.

The single most important practical rule of malware analysis is *containment* of the analysis itself: malware must be analyzed only in a properly isolated environment, deliberately separated from production systems and from the network, because running live malware is exactly the dangerous act you are trying to defend against. An analysis environment that is not truly isolated can become the source of the very outbreak it was meant to study. This is specialist work, and most organizations do not perform deep reverse engineering themselves. They rely on the analysis built into their security products, on threat-intelligence services, and on external specialists, while doing lighter triage in-house. But understanding what the discipline is and what it produces matters even if you never disassemble a sample yourself, because the indicators it yields drive detection and eradication, the timeline it reconstructs informs the breach notification, and the understanding it provides of how the malware operates feeds directly back into the defenses: the signatures, the firewall rules, and the monitoring that stop the next instance. Malware analysis is, in the end, how the defender turns the attacker's own tool into the intelligence that defeats it.

Chapter 15: Network Protocols, Architecture, and Common Attacks

IN THIS CHAPTER

Returning to the wire

The firewall chapters treated the network as a thing to divide into zones and inspect at the boundaries. This chapter goes a layer beneath that, to the protocols and devices that actually move traffic, because many of the most effective and enduring attacks happen not at the application the firewall inspects but in the plumbing underneath: the switches, the address-resolution and address-assignment protocols, and the wireless links. A firewall watching traffic between zones may never look there. Understanding this plumbing is what lets you recognize an attack that does not announce itself as one, and it rounds out the network defense that the earlier chapters began.

A layered model of communication

Network communication is built in layers, each wrapping the one above it in its own envelope, and two models describe these layers. The older conceptual model divides communication into seven layers from the physical wires at the bottom up through the application at the top; the model that actually describes the internet collapses these into four. The details of the models matter less than the habit of mind they instill: that a single piece of traffic is simultaneously a physical signal, a frame addressed between adjacent devices, a packet addressed across the whole internet, a segment belonging to a transport session, and application content. An attacker, and a defender, can operate at any of these levels. A firewall reasoning about applications operates high in the stack; an attacker poisoning address resolution operates low, beneath the firewall's usual gaze, which is exactly why low-layer attacks are so insidious.

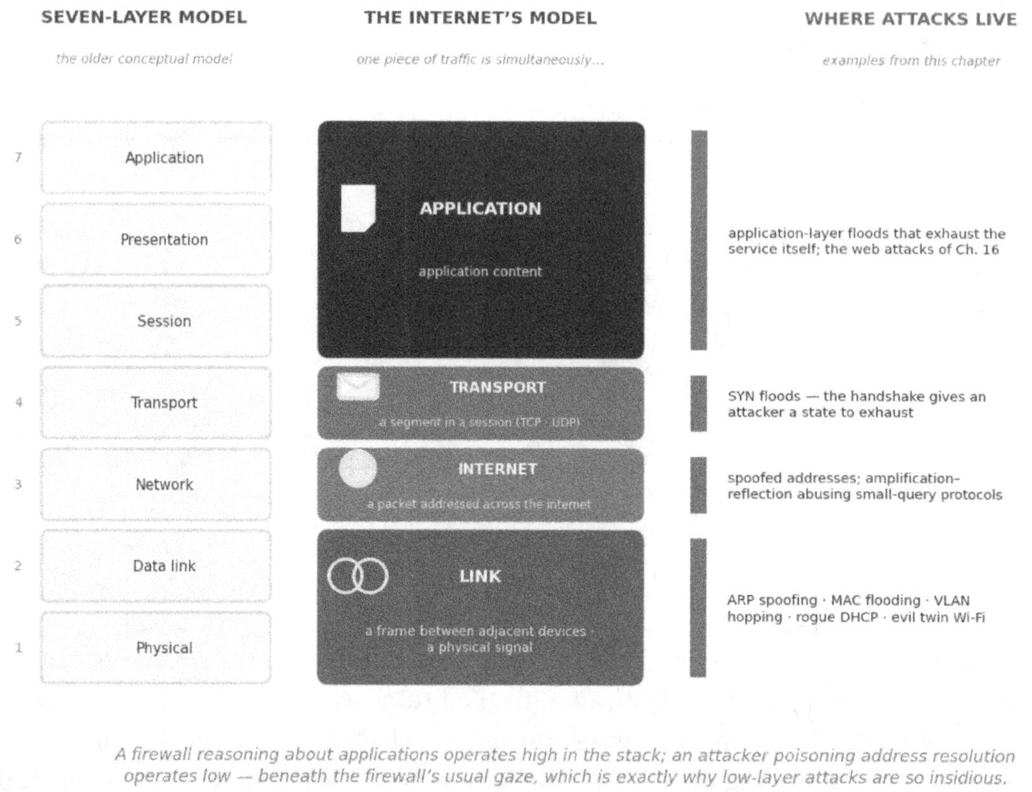

FIGURE 15.1 The layered models — seven conceptual layers, the internet's four, and where this chapter's attacks live.

At the layer that crosses the internet, traffic is addressed by *IP addresses* and divided into *networks* and *subnetworks*. Within a single local network, devices communicate at a lower layer using *hardware addresses*, the MAC addresses burned into network interfaces, and the translation between the two is itself a protocol that, as we will see, is a favorite target. Above the addressing sits the *transport layer*, where TCP provides reliable, ordered, connection-oriented delivery established through a recognizable three-step handshake, while UDP provides fast, connectionless delivery with no handshake and no guarantees. This distinction recurs throughout attacks and defenses, because the TCP handshake both gives a firewall a connection to track and gives an attacker a state to exhaust.

Switching, VLANs, and their attacks

Within a local network, *switches* move frames between devices by learning which hardware address sits on which physical port and forwarding accordingly, maintaining a table of these mappings. This efficiency is also a weakness. In a *MAC flooding attack*, an adversary overwhelms the switch's address table with a flood of fabricated addresses until the table is full. Many switches respond by failing open, broadcasting traffic out all ports as a primitive hub would, which lets the attacker eavesdrop on traffic that should never have reached them. The defense, *port security*, limits how many addresses a port will learn and shuts the port down if the limit is exceeded.

Switched networks are commonly divided into *virtual LANs (VLANs)*. A VLAN takes a single physical switch, or a group of connected switches, and splits it into several separate logical networks that cannot directly reach one another, even though they share the same hardware. This is how the segmentation discussed in earlier chapters is actually implemented at the switching layer: instead of buying separate switches for the finance team, the engineering team, and the guest Wi-Fi, an organization configures one set of switches to behave as if it were several.

When traffic for multiple VLANs needs to travel between switches, it moves across a special connection called a *trunk link*. Because a trunk carries traffic from many VLANs at once, each frame is given a small tag that identifies which VLAN it belongs to, so the switch on the other end knows where to deliver it.

Attackers target this arrangement with a class of attacks called *VLAN hopping*. In one version, the attacker tricks a switch into treating the attacker's device as if it were another switch, opening a trunk link to it. Once a trunk is established, the attacker can see and send traffic for every VLAN that trunk carries. In another version, the attacker exploits the way some switches handle frames that carry two VLAN tags stacked together, slipping traffic into a VLAN they were never supposed to reach.

The defenses are matters of careful switch configuration rather than fancy technology. Trunk links should never be established automatically; they should be set up deliberately by an administrator. Every switch port should be assigned explicitly to the VLAN it belongs to, rather than left to negotiate on its own. Sensitive traffic should never be placed on the *default VLAN* that switches use out of the box, because that VLAN is the easiest one for an attacker to land on by accident or by design. The broader lesson is that segmentation at this layer is only as strong as the switch configuration beneath it. A misconfigured switch can quietly undo all of the network design above it.

Address resolution and its poisoning

When a computer wants to send a frame to another device on the same local network, it cannot use the IP address directly. At this layer, devices identify each other by hardware address, the unique identifier burned into each network card. So the sender needs to figure out which hardware address goes with the IP address it is trying to reach. It does this using the *Address Resolution Protocol (ARP)*. The sender shouts a broadcast onto the network asking "who has this IP address?" and waits for a reply. Whichever device answers is trusted, and the sender records the answer in a table so it does not have to ask again for a while.

That trust is the flaw, because ARP has no way to verify that the device answering is really the device it claims to be. In an attack called *ARP spoofing*, sometimes called *ARP poisoning*, the attacker answers these requests falsely. For example, when a device on the network asks "who has the IP address of the gateway?" the attacker replies "I do," giving its own hardware address. The victim updates its table accordingly and begins sending the attacker any traffic that was meant for the gateway. The attacker now sits in the middle of the conversation, a position known as *man-in-the-middle*, and can eavesdrop on the traffic, alter it, or harvest credentials. The firewall never sees the attack, because the whole thing happens beneath it on the local network. This is one of the classic local-network attacks for exactly this reason: ARP simply believes whatever answer it receives. The defense is called *dynamic ARP inspection*, in which the switch checks ARP messages against a trusted record of which hardware address goes with which IP address and drops the forgeries. Once again, the remedy is located in the switch itself.

Address assignment and its abuse

When a device first joins a network, it usually does not have any address configuration of its own and needs the network to provide one. It does this through the *Dynamic Host Configuration Protocol (DHCP)*. The device sends out a request asking for an address, and a DHCP server somewhere on the network answers with a complete configuration: the IP address the device should use, the gateway it should send outbound traffic to, and, importantly, which DNS servers it should consult to look up names. The device accepts this configuration and begins using it.

Like ARP, DHCP trusts the response it gets, and attackers abuse that trust in two ways. In a *rogue DHCP server attack*, an attacker connects their own DHCP server to the network and races to answer requests before the legitimate server does. Victims who accept the attacker's configuration end up with a gateway or DNS server that points back to the attacker, again placing the attacker in a man-in-the-middle position or steering victims to fraudulent sites. In a *DHCP starvation attack*, the attacker floods the legitimate DHCP server with so many fake requests that it exhausts its supply of available addresses and can no longer serve real clients. This is often a setup for the rogue server attack, so that when victims ask for an address, only the attacker's server is left to answer. The defense is called *DHCP snooping*, in which the switch is told which of its ports the legitimate DHCP server is connected to, and any DHCP responses arriving on other ports are dropped.

The pattern across ARP and DHCP is identical and worth absorbing as a single lesson. These foundational local-network protocols were designed in a more trusting era, with no way to verify the answers they receive. Attackers exploit that trust to insert themselves between victims and the rest of the network. The modern defenses, rather than trying to retrofit authentication into the protocols themselves, push validation down into the switches, the only devices positioned to see every frame and to enforce what is allowed where.

Denial of service and distributed denial of service

Not every attack tries to steal information or alter it. Some attacks simply try to make a service unavailable, going directly after the availability leg of the CIA triad. An attack of this kind is called a *denial-of-service attack*, often shortened to *DoS*. The idea is straightforward: overwhelm a target so completely that legitimate users cannot reach it. The website does not technically get broken into, no data gets stolen, but for the people trying to use the service, the outcome is the same as if it had been destroyed. They cannot get in.

When the attack comes from a single source, the target's defenders can often identify and block that source. So attackers escalate by enlisting many machines at once, typically a *botnet* of compromised computers under the attacker's remote control, as described in the threats chapter. An attack launched from many machines simultaneously is called a *distributed denial-of-service attack*, or

DDoS. The distributed nature is what makes it so hard to stop: the flood arrives from thousands or millions of different addresses, often from all over the world, and blocking any single one of them does almost nothing because there are countless others still coming.

DDoS attacks come in several distinct flavors, and it is worth understanding the differences because the defenses against each are different.

Volumetric attacks are the most straightforward. The attacker simply floods the target's network connection with more traffic than it can carry. The legitimate traffic is not blocked by any clever mechanism; it is just drowned in sheer volume, the way a normal conversation becomes impossible inside a packed and noisy stadium.

Protocol attacks are sneakier. Rather than overwhelming the network connection, they target and exhaust a specific resource the target depends on to function. The classic example is the *SYN flood*: the attacker sends a barrage of opening requests for new TCP connections, the first step of the three-way handshake that begins every TCP conversation, but never sends the third step that would complete those connections. The server, dutifully holding each half-open connection in memory while it waits for the missing step, eventually fills its table of pending connections and cannot accept any new ones, legitimate or otherwise.

Application-layer attacks are subtler still. The attacker sends requests that look legitimate on the surface but are deliberately crafted to consume far more of the application's resources than a normal request would. A request that triggers a complex database query, for example, or one that asks the server to do an unusually expensive piece of work, can exhaust the application itself with comparatively little traffic, slipping under defenses that are watching for raw volume.

A particularly potent technique is called *amplification*, also known as *reflection*. The attacker takes advantage of two things at once. First, certain kinds of servers on the public internet, often misconfigured DNS resolvers, time servers, or other services that anyone can query, will respond to small requests with much larger responses. Second, some of the protocols these servers use do not verify where a request actually came from. The attacker exploits both by sending a flood of small requests to these servers while forging the source address on each request to make it look as if it came from the victim. The servers, having no way to know better, dutifully send their much larger responses to the victim. The attacker has now turned a modest stream of outbound traffic into a massive flood arriving at the victim, and hidden their own identity behind a crowd of innocent intermediaries who never knew they were participating in an attack.

Defending against denial-of-service attacks is partly a contest of scale that a single firewall cannot win. The problem is that a large enough flood can saturate the internet connection the firewall sits behind before the firewall has any chance to do its job. If the pipe coming into the building is full of attack traffic, it does not matter how clever the firewall is at filtering; the legitimate traffic cannot get through the congestion to reach it.

The practical defenses therefore have to reach upstream, beyond the organization's own perimeter. *Rate limiting* and filtering can be applied at the network edge, where the organization's network meets its internet provider, blocking obvious attack traffic before it consumes the connection.

Services can be distributed across many locations, so that no single site has to absorb the entire flood on its own. Most commonly, for organizations with serious exposure, specialized *cloud-based DDoS protection services* can be hired to sit far out in the network, absorbing and scrubbing attack traffic before it ever reaches the organization's connection at all.

This is one of the clearer cases in security where the right control lives outside your own walls, because the problem is bigger than your walls can hold. A firewall, no matter how well configured, cannot defend against a flood that arrives before the firewall does.

Controlling who joins the network

The attacks above mostly assume the adversary can already put a device on the network. That raises the question of how you control that in the first place. *Network access control (NAC)* governs which devices are allowed to connect at all.

The standard mechanism is built on a protocol called *802.1X*, and the rule is simple: a device must prove who it is before the switch or wireless access point will grant it any real network access. Until that proof arrives, the port stays closed to everything except the authentication exchange itself. A device that plugs into a conference-room jack or associates with the Wi-Fi cannot yet send or receive normal traffic. It can only participate in the conversation that decides whether it belongs.

That conversation involves three parties. The device trying to connect, such as a laptop, phone, or printer, is the *supplicant*. The switch port or wireless access point it is connecting through is the *authenticator*, the gatekeeper that physically controls whether the device gets through. Somewhere on the network sits an *authentication server*, typically a RADIUS server, which holds the actual list of who is allowed. The authenticator passes the device's credentials to the authentication server, the server replies yes or no, and the authenticator either opens the port or keeps it closed. The credentials can be a username and password, but in serious deployments they are usually certificates installed on managed devices, which are stronger and tie access to a specific corporate device rather than to a credential that could be stolen.

Not every device can play this game. Printers, IP cameras, badge readers, and many building sensors speak only the basic networking protocols and cannot perform 802.1X at all. The workaround is a fallback called *MAC authentication bypass (MAB)*, in which the switch identifies the device by its hardware address and looks it up in a list of pre-approved devices. MAB is weaker than 802.1X because hardware addresses can be forged, so the practice is to confine these devices to restricted segments where they can do their job but cannot reach sensitive systems. A printer never needs to talk to the finance database, and the network should refuse to carry that traffic even if the printer is somehow impersonated.

Modern NAC does more than decide yes or no at the door. Once a device's identity is established, the NAC system can check its health: is the operating system patched, is the required antivirus running, is the disk encrypted, is the device managed by the corporate device-management system? Devices that fall short can be quarantined to a remediation segment where they can download patches but cannot reach production, restricted to a guest-style segment with internet access only, or denied entirely. Different kinds of devices can also be steered onto different VLANs automatically: the engineering laptop to the engineering VLAN, the contractor's laptop to the contractor VLAN, and the unknown device nowhere useful. This is the *device-posture checking* and *dynamic segmentation* the zero-trust chapter described, enforced at the earliest possible moment: the moment of physical or wireless connection.

NAC extends the identity-centric thinking of the earlier chapters down to the layer where wires meet jacks and radios meet antennas. An attacker who plugs into a conference-room jack or associates with the Wi-Fi no longer gets a free ride. They have to prove who they are, prove the device is healthy, and even then they only get access to what their identity allows. Verify everything, trust nothing by default, applied to the network's plumbing.

Wireless security

Wireless networks deserve particular attention because they extend the network into the air, where an attacker need not plug into anything. They need only be within range, often outside the building entirely. The encryption protecting Wi-Fi has evolved through generations, and the practical guidance is to use the current generation and to retire the older ones, whose weaknesses are well documented and actively exploited. An access point still running a long-obsolete protocol is an open door dressed as a locked one.

Beyond the encryption itself, wireless networks face distinctive attacks. A *rogue access point* is an unauthorized device attached to the network, sometimes planted by an attacker and sometimes innocently added by an employee wanting better coverage, that creates an uncontrolled entry point bypassing the perimeter entirely. An *evil twin* is an access point impersonating a legitimate one, luring devices and users into connecting to the attacker so that all their traffic flows through the attacker's hands. *Deauthentication attacks* forcibly disconnect devices, both as a denial of service and to drive victims toward an evil twin.

Sound wireless security combines several measures. Use strong, current encryption, and for organizational networks prefer enterprise authentication built on 802.1X, where each user authenticates individually against the identity system rather than everyone sharing one password, so that access can be granted and revoked per person exactly as elsewhere. Segregate untrusted wireless, guest networks above all, onto isolated segments that cannot reach internal systems, applying the segmentation principles of the architecture chapters so that a guest's compromised laptop reaches nothing of value. Monitor for rogue and impersonating access points with *wireless intrusion detection*, since the rogue device announces itself to anyone listening. Treat the wireless network, like the VPN, as an extension of the network into hostile territory that must be authenticated, encrypted, and segmented rather than implicitly trusted because it is "ours."

TABLE 15.1 Network and wireless attacks, and the defenses that answer them

Attack	What it does	The defense
MAC flooding	Overwhelms a switch's address table so it floods traffic out of every port, letting an attacker eavesdrop	Port security to limit the addresses a port will learn
VLAN hopping	Tricks a switch into carrying the attacker's traffic onto VLANs they should not reach	Explicit trunk configuration; never auto-negotiate trunking
ARP spoofing / poisoning	Forges address-resolution replies so traffic for another host flows through the attacker	Dynamic ARP inspection, validating replies against trusted bindings
Rogue DHCP and starvation	A false server hands out attacker-controlled network settings, or exhausts the address pool	DHCP snooping so only trusted ports may answer
DoS / DDoS — volumetric	Floods the connection with more traffic than it can carry, from one source or a botnet's many	Upstream and cloud-scale mitigation — the control lives outside your own walls
DoS — protocol (SYN flood)	Exhausts a specific resource — half-open TCP connections that never complete the handshake	SYN protections and rate limiting at the edge
DoS — application-layer	Legitimate-looking requests crafted to consume disproportionate resources	Application-aware filtering; watch resource cost, not just volume
Amplification / reflection	Small forged-source queries to public servers (often DNS) so much larger replies flood the victim	Provider-level filtering; close open amplifiers
Rogue access point	An unauthorized device attached to the network, extending it to attackers	Wireless monitoring and network access control
Evil twin	A look-alike wireless network that lures users into connecting through the attacker	Enterprise authentication; user awareness; wireless intrusion detection
Deauthentication	Forged management frames knock clients off the legitimate network, often to capture reconnection	Protected management frames and wireless intrusion detection

The foundational protocols — ARP, DHCP, the early wireless standards — were designed for cooperative networks and assume honesty; the defenses retrofit verification onto trusting designs.

The recurring lesson beneath the network

Step back from the specific attacks and a single lesson emerges across all of them. The foundational network protocols, including ARP, DHCP, the early wireless standards, and the trust between switches, were designed in an era that assumed the participants were honest. Nearly every attack in this chapter is an abuse of that built-in trust by an adversary the protocols never anticipated. The modern defenses, correspondingly, are all variations on a single theme: replace blind trust with verification, pushed down to the lowest layer where the trust was being abused. That means validating ARP, snooping DHCP, authenticating devices before they join, encrypting and authenticating the wireless link, and segmenting so that abuse in one place cannot spread. This is the same shift from implicit to verified trust that defines zero trust at the higher layers, applied to the plumbing, and it is why a defender who understands the network beneath the firewall can catch and prevent attacks that the firewall alone would never see. The network is not a neutral medium that security sits on top of; it is itself a contested space, and defending it is part of the job.

Chapter 16: Endpoint, Application, and Data Security

IN THIS CHAPTER

Where attacks actually land and what they actually want
Securing the endpoint
Web application security
Building security into development
Protecting the data itself

Where attacks actually land and what they actually want

Two truths bracket this chapter. Attacks overwhelmingly land on *endpoints*, the laptops, desktops, servers, and phones where users click links, open files, and run programs, because that is where people are, and people are the most reliable way in. Attacks ultimately want data, or the applications that hold and process it. The earlier chapters defended the network between these two points; this chapter defends the points themselves, the endpoints where compromise begins and the applications and data that are its destination. A defense that secures the network but neglects the endpoint and the application has fortified the hallway while leaving the rooms unlocked.

Securing the endpoint

An endpoint is exposed to threats the network controls cannot fully stop: the user who opens a malicious attachment, the browser that visits a compromised site, and the program downloaded from somewhere untrustworthy. *Endpoint hardening* reduces this exposure through the same principles seen throughout the book, applied to the individual machine. Keep the operating system and applications patched, since the endpoint is a prime target for the known-vulnerability exploitation the vulnerability chapter described. Remove unnecessary software and disable unneeded services and features, shrinking the attack surface of each machine. Critically, remove *local administrator rights* from ordinary users, so that a compromise through a user's everyday activity does not immediately hand the attacker full control of the machine. This is an application of least privilege at the endpoint that blunts a large fraction of malware, which relies on the privileges of the account that runs it. Enable the *host firewall* so that each machine enforces its own restrictions on what may connect to it, a layer of defense that persists even when the network's segmentation is bypassed. Enable *full-disk encryption*, the data-at-rest control that turns a lost or stolen device from a data breach into a mere inconvenience, as the encryption and incident chapters both stressed.

The tools that protect endpoints have evolved markedly. *Traditional antivirus* matched files against signatures of known malware, which was useful but, like all signature approaches, blind to the novel and increasingly evaded by the fileless and obfuscated techniques of the malware chapter. *Endpoint detection and response (EDR)* represents a substantial advance. Rather than only matching known-bad files, it continuously records detailed endpoint activity, including processes, file changes, network connections, and registry changes. It watches for the behaviors that indicate an attack regardless of whether the specific malware is known, and it enables both rapid response, such as isolating a compromised machine from the network at a click, and after-the-fact investigation by replaying what happened. The further evolution, *extended detection and response (XDR)*, correlates these endpoint signals with network, email, and cloud telemetry, embodying the recurring principle that more vantage points, correlated, beat any single one. A complementary and powerful control for high-security environments is *application allowlisting*, which permits only explicitly approved programs to run and blocks everything else by default. This is the default-deny philosophy of the firewall applied to software execution, and it is a strong defense against malware because unapproved code simply cannot run, though it demands discipline to maintain as legitimate software changes.

Web application security

A great deal of the world's valuable data sits behind web applications, which are exposed to the entire internet by design and are therefore among the most relentlessly attacked surfaces in existence. *Web application security* is a discipline in its own right, but its most common vulnerabilities share a single root cause worth understanding deeply, because grasping the root teaches the whole category: the application trusting input it should not trust. Almost every classic web vulnerability is a variation on untrusted input being treated as if it were safe.

The canonical example is *injection*, most famously *SQL injection*, in which an attacker supplies input crafted so that the application's database treats part of it as a command rather than as data. This allows the attacker to read, alter, or destroy the database by smuggling instructions inside what should have been a harmless value like a search term or a username. The defense is to never mix untrusted input into a command, achieved through *parameterized queries* that keep data and command rigorously separate. The same principle defeats injection into other interpreters as well.

A second pervasive class is *cross-site scripting*, in which an attacker gets their own script embedded into a page that other users view, so that the script runs in those victims' browsers with the victims' access, stealing sessions, capturing keystrokes, or acting as the user. Its defense is to treat all user-supplied content as untrusted when displaying it, encoding it so the browser renders it as inert text rather than executing it as code.

A third major class is *broken access control*, in which the application fails to properly enforce what each user is allowed to do or see. A user may be able to reach another user's data simply by altering a reference, or perform actions they should not be permitted. This is the failure of authorization that the identity chapter warned must be enforced rigorously and on the server, never merely hidden in the interface.

Rounding out the common risks are *broken authentication and session management*, *security misconfiguration* such as default credentials and needlessly exposed features, exposure of sensitive data through inadequate encryption, *server-side request forgery* in which the application is tricked into making requests on the attacker's behalf, the use of components with known vulnerabilities drawn from the software supply chain, and *insufficient logging and monitoring* that lets attacks proceed unseen. This is the very gap the operations chapter exists to close.

TABLE 16.1 Common web-application attacks and their primary defenses

Attack class	What goes wrong	Primary defense
Injection (SQL injection)	Attacker-supplied input is executed as database commands, exposing or altering data wholesale	Parameterized queries — keep data and commands strictly separate; validate input
Cross-site scripting (XSS)	The attacker's script gets embedded into a page other users view and runs in their browsers	Output encoding and strict handling of untrusted content
Broken access control	The application fails to enforce what each user may do or see — e.g., changing an ID in a URL exposes someone else's data	Enforce authorization server-side on every request; never trust the client
Broken authentication and session management	Weak login and session handling let attackers take over accounts	Strong authentication, careful session handling, and modern frameworks' protections
Security misconfiguration	Default credentials, insecure authentication, excessive permissions, weak authorization, exposed endpoints, improperly secured connections between services and APIs	Scan for vulnerabilities and exposed ports and services and hardened to minimize exposure and attack surface. Ensure configuration hygiene and apply least privileged principle
Sensitive data exposure	Data unprotected in transit or at rest leaks when something else fails	Encryption in transit and at rest, per the encryption chapter

The durable defense is secure development; a web application firewall adds a protective layer but does not substitute for fixing the application itself.

Defending web applications operates at two levels. The durable, fundamental defense is *secure development*: writing the application so that it validates input, separates data from commands, enforces access control on the server, encrypts sensitive data, and is built on maintained, patched components. A vulnerability that is never written cannot be exploited. The complementary defense is the *web application firewall (WAF)*, a specialized firewall that inspects the application-layer traffic to and from a web application and blocks common attack patterns such as injection and cross-site scripting attempts. The web application firewall is genuinely valuable, especially as a shield that buys time when a vulnerability is discovered but cannot be fixed immediately, but it is a complement to secure development and never a substitute for it. Relying on the web application firewall while shipping insecure code is patching the symptom while leaving the disease, and a determined attacker will eventually find the request the filter does not catch. The same caution applies to the proliferating world of *application programming interfaces (APIs)*, through which applications and services talk to one another and which now carry an enormous share of sensitive data. APIs face the same input-trust and access-control failures as web pages, often with less scrutiny, and they must be authenticated, authorized, validated, and rate-limited with the same rigor.

Building security into development

Because secure development is the durable defense, mature organizations build security into the software development process itself rather than testing for it only at the end. This approach is often called *DevSecOps*: integrating security throughout development and deployment rather than bolting it on, the shift-left principle of the deployment chapter applied to building software. This means several concrete practices woven into how software is made.

Threat modeling during design asks how the thing being built could be attacked, while the answers can still shape the design cheaply. *Secure coding practices* and developer training reduce the rate at which vulnerabilities are written in the first place. Automated analysis catches flaws early: *static analysis* examines the source code for vulnerable patterns without running it, *dynamic analysis* tests the running application by probing it as an attacker would, and *software composition analysis* checks the third-party and open-source components the application depends on for known vulnerabilities, addressing the supply-chain risk that the program chapter flagged. *Secrets management* ensures that passwords, keys, and tokens are not hard-coded into source code where they leak, a depressingly common and serious mistake, but held in protected stores. This applies the key-management discipline of the encryption chapter to all credentials. The pipeline that builds and deploys the software must itself be secured, because an attacker who compromises the build process can insert malicious code into everything it produces, a supply-chain attack against the organization's own software.

A note on the increasingly common practice of packaging applications into *containers* and orchestrating them at scale: this brings real benefits but its own security considerations. The container images must be built from trusted, patched bases and scanned for vulnerabilities, the *orchestration platform* must be configured and access-controlled carefully, and the same isolation and least-privilege thinking applies to containers as to any other workload, with microsegmentation often enforced at this layer.

Protecting the data itself

All of this ultimately serves the protection of data, and it is worth gathering the data-specific controls that have appeared throughout the book into one place, because data is the asset and everything else is in service of it. It begins with *classification*, the sorting of data by sensitivity from the assets chapter, because every other data control depends on knowing what matters most. *Encryption* protects data in transit and at rest, the backstop that limits the damage when other controls fail, and rests on the key management that determines whether the encryption is real. *Access control*, grounded in least privilege and the identity chapter, ensures only the right people and systems can reach each piece of data. *Integrity controls*, including cryptographic hashes, digital signatures, and write-once storage for records that must not be altered, protect against silent tampering, so that data not only stays confidential but stays correct.

Data loss prevention watches for sensitive data leaving where it should not. *Database security* applies hardening, least privilege, encryption, and monitoring to the repositories where structured data concentrates, and treats the database's own accounts and default credentials as the high-value targets they are. *Backups*, maintained, isolated, and tested, protect against the destruction and ransomware that threaten availability and integrity. *Secure disposal* ensures that data is genuinely destroyed when no longer needed, wiped from drives or rendered unrecoverable by destroying the keys that decrypt it, a technique called *crypto-shredding*, rather than lingering on discarded equipment to be recovered by whoever finds it, closing the lifecycle that classification opened.

Perhaps the most underused control is the simplest: *data minimization*. The data you never collect, or that you delete once its purpose is served, is data that cannot be breached, and reducing the data you hold simultaneously lowers risk and eases the regulatory burden of the data-protection chapter. The endpoint is where attacks begin and the application is where they operate, but the data is what they are for, and a security program is ultimately judged by whether the data it was built to protect stayed confidential, intact, and available.

Chapter 17: Artificial Intelligence in Security

IN THIS CHAPTER

A tool for both sides

Artificial intelligence has arrived in security from three directions at once, and clear thinking requires keeping them separate: AI as a help to defenders, AI as a weapon for attackers, and AI systems as a new kind of thing that itself must be secured. None of these is magic, and the breathless framing on all sides, that AI will solve security or that AI will end it, is marketing rather than analysis. The grounded view is that AI is a powerful tool that shifts the balance in specific, identifiable ways on both offense and defense, while introducing a genuinely new attack surface of its own that traditional practices do not fully cover. A professional engages with all three soberly, neither dismissing the technology as hype nor surrendering judgment to it.

AI as a help to defenders

The defensive applications are real and largely incremental rather than revolutionary, which is not a criticism. Incremental improvements compound. AI, and *machine learning* in particular, is well suited to the pattern-finding at the heart of detection: sifting enormous volumes of logs and network traffic to surface the anomalies a human analyst would never have time to find, which is why it increasingly powers the anomaly-based detection and behavioral analysis behind the monitoring of the operations chapter. It helps directly with the alert-fatigue problem by triaging and correlating alerts, suppressing the obvious noise and surfacing what merits human attention, and it powers much of the automation in SOAR playbooks. It can accelerate an incident responder's work by rapidly summarizing what happened across scattered systems, assembling a timeline from fragments that would take a human hours to piece together. It also assists in spotting the subtle behavioral shifts, such as a user account suddenly acting unlike itself or a system communicating in a new pattern, that signal a compromised insider or a stolen credential.

Beyond the operations center, AI is finding its way into nearly every part of a security program. It accelerates threat intelligence work by ingesting feeds from dozens of sources, deduplicating and correlating indicators across them, and connecting external intelligence to the organization's own environment, so that analysts see the threats that actually matter rather than drowning in everything published anywhere. It supports proactive threat hunting, helping analysts formulate hypotheses, search vast historical data for patterns matching known adversary techniques, and surface activity that did not trip any alert but warrants a closer look. This can turn hunting from an artisanal craft that only the best-funded teams could afford into a discipline that more organizations can practice. It strengthens email security, where machine-learning models at the gateway identify phishing attempts not by static signatures but by analyzing tone, sender behavior, link characteristics, and the overall context of a message, catching attacks that would have slipped past older filters. It helps with vulnerability management by correlating disclosed weaknesses to the organization's actual exposure: what is installed, what is reachable, and what is being actively exploited in the wild. That lets patching effort go where it matters most rather than being spread evenly across a backlog. It also lightens the burden of documentation and communication, summarizing scattered findings into readable reports, drafting incident write-ups, and translating technical detail into the language different audiences need, freeing analysts to spend their time on the parts of the work that actually require their expertise.

The honest qualification, which matters enormously, is that these tools augment rather than replace skilled people. They generate leads, not verdicts, and an over-reliance on them, treating their output as truth rather than as a prioritized starting point for human judgment, reintroduces the same complacency that any single control invites. AI systems can be confidently wrong, can be fooled, and can miss the genuinely novel attack that does not resemble their training. The right posture is to let AI do what it is good at, which is tireless pattern-matching at scale, while keeping experienced humans in the loop for the judgment, context, and skepticism that the technology cannot supply. The security function that fires its analysts because it bought an AI tool has misunderstood both the tool and the work.

AI as a weapon for attackers

The same capabilities serve attackers, and pretending otherwise is naïve. AI makes social engineering markedly more effective. Phishing messages that once betrayed themselves through clumsy grammar and awkward phrasing can now be fluent, personalized, and produced at scale in any language, eroding the old advice to spot phishing by its mistakes. The same technology generates convincing fake audio and video, known as *deepfakes*, that have already been used to impersonate executives and authorize fraudulent transfers, putting a familiar face and voice behind a fraud in a way that defeats the human instinct to trust what we see and hear. AI can also assist in generating and mutating malware to evade signature-based detection, producing endless variants of the same underlying threat.

A newer and more troubling development is the use of AI not just to draft messages or generate malware but to actually carry out the work of an attack. *Agentic AI* refers to models that can plan, take actions, call tools, observe the results, and decide what to do next. This collapses parts of the attack chain that used to require a skilled human operator. A reconnaissance phase that once took a junior attacker hours of manually probing a target can be handed to an agent that scans the attack surface, reads the results, identifies the most promising weaknesses, and reports back. A vulnerability that would have required a researcher to read documentation, write a proof of concept, and adapt it to the specific environment can increasingly be handed to an agent that does all three. None of this means AI is yet a fully autonomous attacker, and the most capable systems still need human direction at key moments. But the trend line is clear: tasks that used to require expertise and time are being compressed into prompts and minutes, lowering the barrier to entry for capabilities that once filtered out unsophisticated attackers and raising the pace at which sophisticated ones can operate. The same agentic capabilities that let a defender automate triage let an attacker automate intrusion, and the defenders who do not match that pace will fall behind it.

The realistic implication is not panic but a recalibration of certain defenses. The decline of the bad-grammar tell raises the value of the technical controls that do not depend on human judgment, above all the phishing-resistant authentication of the identity chapter, which defeats credential theft regardless of how convincing the lure, and the email authentication of the DNS-and-email chapter, which stops spoofing regardless of how fluent the message. It also raises the value of verification procedures that do not rely on recognizing a familiar voice or face, such as confirming an unusual financial request through a separate, known channel rather than trusting the voice on the phone, because that voice can now be synthesized. The countermeasure to AI-enhanced deception is, in large part, process: controls and verification steps that hold even when the human senses are fooled. The countermeasure to AI-enabled exploitation is, in large part, speed: closing known vulnerabilities before automated discovery finds them, and matching the attacker's automation with defensive automation of patching, detection, and response. These are the fundamentals of the basics chapter, made urgent by an adversary that no longer needs to sleep.

Securing AI systems themselves

The newest and least understood front is that AI systems are software with their own distinctive vulnerabilities, and as organizations rush to deploy them they create attack surface that traditional security practices do not fully address. The most prominent novel weakness is *prompt injection*, in which an attacker hides instructions in content that the AI processes, such as a web page, a document, an email, or a record in a database, causing the system to ignore its intended constraints and follow the attacker's instructions instead. It is, in effect, a way of smuggling commands into a system that cannot reliably distinguish the data it is supposed to process from instructions it is supposed to obey, and it is genuinely hard to eliminate because that ambiguity is close to inherent in how these systems work. Related is *jailbreaking*, crafting inputs that coax a model past its safety guardrails into doing what it was built to refuse.

Beyond manipulating a running system lie attacks on the model itself. *Data poisoning* corrupts the training data so that the model learns harmful or attacker-chosen behavior, a threat that grows as models are trained on vast, hard-to-vet collections of public data. *Model extraction*, or model theft, reconstructs a proprietary model by probing it systematically, stealing the expensive intellectual property embodied in it. *Training-data leakage* coaxes a model into revealing sensitive information it absorbed during training, which matters acutely when models are trained on confidential data. There is also a supply-chain dimension, since models and their components are increasingly pulled from public repositories whose integrity must be considered exactly as with any other software dependency, because a tampered model is as dangerous as tampered code.

A practical governance concern sits alongside these technical ones: *shadow AI*, the use of public AI services by employees who paste sensitive company data into them to get their work done, creating a data-leakage risk that no firewall will catch because the data walks out through an ordinary, sanctioned-looking web connection. This is the cloud-application governance problem of the CASB chapter in a new and fast-spreading form. The response blends old and new. The familiar disciplines apply: treat AI systems as assets to inventory, classify the data they touch, apply least privilege to what they can access and do, monitor their behavior, and include them in your threat modeling. New practices specific to this domain are maturing alongside those familiar disciplines. Treat all input to a model as untrusted, much as a web application must treat all user input as hostile. Constrain what an AI system is permitted to do and access so that a successful injection has a limited blast radius, which is least privilege applied to an agent that may be manipulated. Establish clear policy about which AI tools may be used with which categories of data. Published guidance specific to AI risks, such as the community-maintained lists of top vulnerabilities for applications built on large language models, is a sensible reference as the field's practices solidify. At the program level, the *NIST AI Risk Management Framework* introduced among the domain frameworks of the risk chapter offers a structured way to govern these risks through its govern, map, measure, and manage functions.

What is harder to overstate is how quickly this landscape is changing, and the most important habit a security program can build around AI is the habit of staying current with it. New attack techniques against AI systems appear monthly, the models themselves are revised on similar timescales, and the controls that work today may not be the controls that work in a year. This argues for several disciplines worth naming explicitly. Patch quickly: when the maintainer of a model, framework, or AI platform publishes a fix, the window between disclosure and exploitation is often short, and the slow patching cycles that organizations have tolerated for traditional software are not safe to extend to this domain. Watch the research: the open security-research community, academic conferences, and the safety-and-alignment teams at the major AI providers publish a steady stream of new findings, and a designated person or small team should be tracking that flow rather than letting the organization learn about new attack classes by experiencing them. Test continuously: red-team the AI systems the organization deploys, both internally and through external assessments, because the threat model evolves and a one-time security review ages quickly. Keep policy living: the rules about which AI tools may be used with which data should be reviewed regularly rather than set once and forgotten, because both the tools and their risk profiles change. Build the relationships now that the organization will need later: with legal teams as regulation matures, with the providers of the AI services in use so that incidents can be escalated quickly, and with peer organizations whose lessons learned will reach you faster than the next breach report. The prudent organization neither bans AI outright, which merely drives it into the shadows where it cannot be governed, nor adopts it uncritically, which imports its risks wholesale. It engages with AI deliberately, capturing the benefit while managing the new exposure, and accepts that "deliberately" means continuously, because the ground beneath this technology will keep moving for the foreseeable future.

The enduring discipline beneath the new technology

It is worth observing that the two forces most reshaping the field, artificial intelligence and the quantum computing of the encryption chapter, share a common lesson for the practitioner: both are areas of rapid change and genuine uncertainty where the right posture is preparation and agility rather than either panic or dismissal. For AI, that means deploying it where it genuinely helps, defending against its use by attackers, and securing the AI systems you adopt. For quantum, it means building *crypto-agility* now so you can adapt when the standards and the threat mature. In both cases, the enduring fundamentals of this book remain the foundation on which any response to the new must be built: reason honestly about risk, layer your defenses, keep the unglamorous basics in good order, and prepare for the incident you cannot prevent. The technologies change, sometimes dramatically; the discipline does not. An organization grounded in the fundamentals will absorb each new wave, adapting its tools while keeping its judgment, and that adaptability rooted in principle is worth more than any specific technology, because the next disruption is always coming and the principles are what carry across it.

Afterword

Cybersecurity is not mainly a collection of tools. It is a way of thinking about risk, trust, failure, and adversaries. The tools change, the threats evolve, and the products that seem essential today may seem ordinary or outdated in a few years. What endures is the discipline: understand what the organization is trying to protect, reason honestly about risk, layer defenses so no single failure is fatal, watch for the failures that will come anyway, keep the fundamentals in good order, and prepare for the incident you cannot fully prevent.

Throughout this book, we have studied a great deal of machinery: firewalls, encryption, authentication, network design, zero trust, cloud-delivered security, monitoring, incident response, and malware analysis. Each topic matters, but none of them stands alone. Again and again, the technical details returned to the same underlying principles: least privilege, defense in depth, default deny, attack-surface reduction, risk management, and the humility to assume that even well-designed systems can fail. The sophistication of modern security is in service of those principles, not a replacement for them. A practitioner who masters the tools but forgets the principles may build elegant controls that protect the wrong things.

You will not make anything perfectly secure. No one ever has, and the claim to have done so is usually a sign that someone does not understand the problem. Security work is not about eliminating all risk. It is about reducing risk intelligently, repeatedly, and in ways that support the people and missions behind the systems. Done well, that work changes the odds. It prevents breaches that never make the news, protects data that is never stolen, and preserves trust that no one notices because it was never broken.

Much of this work is invisible. Prevented disasters leave no dramatic evidence behind. The network keeps running. The customer keeps trusting. The agency keeps serving. The business keeps operating. The security professional learns to take quiet satisfaction in that kind of success. That is the work. It is difficult, imperfect, and often unseen. It is also worth doing well.

Appendix: A Working Reference

This appendix distills the book into reference material you can return to without rereading. The reasoning behind each item lives in the chapters above.

A checklist for analyzing any security problem

Identify the asset and what it is worth. Identify the threats, external and internal, human and otherwise. Identify the vulnerabilities in technology, process, and people. Assess the risk as likelihood combined with impact, and make your assumptions explicit and written. Lay out the options: mitigate, transfer, accept, or avoid. Weigh each one's cost against its benefit. Recommend, naming the trade-offs honestly rather than hiding them. Then revisit the decision later, because risk changes as the world does and a sound judgment can quietly become a stale one.

The highest-value controls, roughly in order of protection per unit of effort

Deploy multi-factor authentication everywhere it is supported, ideally phishing-resistant, because it defeats the largest single class of attacks for modest cost. Maintain an accurate asset inventory, because you cannot protect, patch, or monitor what you do not know exists. Patch promptly and manage vulnerabilities by real, contextual risk rather than raw severity score. Maintain and actually test backups, kept isolated enough to survive the event that destroys the originals, because an untested backup is a guess. Apply least privilege to accounts and access, and deprovision leavers reliably. Segment the network so that a single foothold does not become the whole environment. Centralize logging and actually monitor it. Harden systems and relentlessly reduce the attack surface. Configure SPF, DKIM, and an enforced DMARC policy on every domain that sends mail, and use protective DNS filtering. Train people continuously and without blame, building a culture in which mistakes are reported rather than hidden.

Quick reference: firewalls and network defense

A firewall enforces boundaries by deciding what traffic may pass between zones. Configure it default-deny, keep rules narrow and documented, order them so that broad permissive rules do not shadow specific restrictive ones, and review the rule base regularly to prune what has gone stale. Choose a deployment mode to suit the insertion: tap for pure observation, virtual wire or transparent for inline enforcement with minimal disruption, and routed for full capability. Deploy in high-availability pairs with session synchronization so the firewall is not a single point of failure. Understand NAT and PAT and how address translation relates to where the security policy is evaluated.

A next-generation firewall adds identification of the true application regardless of port, identification of the user behind the traffic, and content inspection through security profiles for malware, exploits, file types, data loss, and URL category. These turn policy into the meaningful language of users and applications rather than the brittle language of ports. Keep its threat-intelligence feeds and signatures current, or it decays toward a crude packet filter. Intrusion detection and prevention watch traffic and hosts for attacks using both signatures and anomaly detection, on both the network and key hosts. VPNs protect data crossing untrusted networks; use modern protocols, require strong multi-factor authentication, constrain access, and patch the gateways, which are prime targets. Data loss prevention guards the exits and is strong against accidental leakage, weaker against determined insiders, and dependent on good data classification. None of these stands alone; they are layers of one design, each covering another's failure.

Quick reference: encrypted traffic and decryption

Most traffic is now encrypted, which protects confidentiality but blinds inspection, and attackers hide malware, command-and-control, and exfiltration inside encryption precisely because it defeats inspection. To restore visibility, a firewall can act as a controlled intermediary, decrypting traffic using a trusted internal certificate authority, inspecting it, and re-encrypting it onward. Decrypt selectively, not universally, with maintained exclusions for sensitive and privacy-protected categories such as banking and healthcare. Develop decryption policy with legal counsel and communicate it clearly, because it deliberately breaks the privacy encryption provides. Protect the internal certificate authority as a crown-jewel secret, size the firewall for the heavy load decryption imposes, validate destination certificates rigorously on users' behalf, and exclude applications that resist interception. Decryption is neither to be avoided nor deployed casually; the judgment is in the difference.

Quick reference: identity and modern architecture

Identity is the new perimeter. Separate authentication (who you are), authorization (what you may do), and accounting (what you did). Require multi-factor authentication, preferring phishing-resistant methods for high-value access. Use single sign-on through a well-protected identity provider, and understand the federation protocols: SAML and OpenID Connect prove identity, while OAuth grants delegated permission. Manage the joiner-mover-leaver lifecycle, automating deprovisioning so orphaned accounts do not linger, and guard privileged accounts with extra rigor through vaulting, just-in-time access, and session recording.

Zero trust means never trusting by network location, verifying every request explicitly, granting least privilege, and assuming breach. Segmentation and microsegmentation contain damage by obstructing lateral movement. SASE delivers networking and security from the cloud edge near the user, bundling secure web gateway, CASB, zero-trust network access, and firewall as a service over an SD-WAN foundation. A CASB governs the cloud applications people actually use, including the shadow IT adopted without approval.

Quick reference: email and DNS records

For any domain that sends mail, publish at minimum SPF (authorized senders), DKIM (cryptographic message signature), and DMARC (enforcement and reporting, rolled out report-only and then tightened progressively to reject). Consider MTA-STS and TLS-RPT for transport encryption, BIMI for verified branding once DMARC is enforced, DANE where DNSSEC supports it, and ARC where mail is forwarded. Protect DNS with DNSSEC for integrity, encrypted resolution for query privacy, protective filtering to block malicious domains, and strong protection of the registrar account against hijacking. Know the common record types: A and AAAA for addresses, CNAME for aliases, MX for mail servers, NS and SOA for delegation and zone administration, TXT for verification and policy, PTR for reverse lookup, CAA for permitted certificate authorities, and SRV for service location.

Quick reference: operations and incident response

Log the right things, centralize the logs beyond an attacker's reach, and retain them long enough to be useful. Monitor and correlate through a SIEM that is continuously tuned, watching for anomalies against a known baseline, and accept that a SIEM without skilled staff to run it detects nothing. Automate routine response through SOAR playbooks to act at machine speed and free people for judgment, reserving automated containment for high-confidence cases.

Manage vulnerabilities by contextual risk, patch on a cadence with an emergency track, test patches before broad deployment, and wrap unpatchable systems in compensating controls. Shift security left into planning, test in an environment that mirrors production, and deploy through change management that allows rollback.

For incidents, prepare and practice before anything happens, with legal and management contacts ready; detect and understand the true scope; contain to stop the spread; eradicate completely, including hidden footholds; recover deliberately from trusted, tested backups; and hold a blameless lessons-learned review. Handle evidence carefully throughout, because you cannot know early whether an incident ends in a quiet fix or in court, and remember that legal notification clocks may start at the moment of discovery. Analyze malware only in a truly isolated environment, combining static analysis (safe, but defeated by obfuscation) with dynamic analysis (cuts through obfuscation, but can be defeated by sandbox evasion) to produce the indicators that drive detection and eradication.

A glossary of key terms

Application identification — a next-generation firewall's ability to determine the true application generating traffic regardless of port or protocol, enabling policy in meaningful terms.

Attack surface — the total set of points where an attacker could try to get in or get data out; smaller is safer, and reducing it improves security while lowering cost.

CASB (cloud access security broker) — a control that gives visibility into and governance over the cloud applications an organization uses, including unsanctioned shadow IT.

CIA triad — confidentiality, integrity, availability; the three outcomes security protects, weighted differently for different systems.

Crypto-agility — designing systems so cryptographic algorithms can be swapped without rebuilding everything; the key to surviving the quantum transition.

Decryption / TLS inspection — a controlled interception that decrypts encrypted traffic for inspection and re-encrypts it onward, restoring the visibility encryption removes, at real costs in privacy, performance, and concentrated risk.

Default deny — the foundational policy stance of permitting only what is explicitly intended and denying everything else.

Defense in depth — layering independent controls so that no single failure leads to compromise.

DKIM / SPF / DMARC — the DNS-published mechanisms that authenticate email: a cryptographic message signature, a list of authorized sending servers, and an enforcement-plus-reporting policy that ties them together with alignment.

DLP (data loss prevention) — controls that detect and stop sensitive data from leaving where it should not; strong against accidents, weaker against determined insiders.

DNSSEC — cryptographic signing of DNS records to guarantee their integrity and authenticity, though not their confidentiality.

Federation — trust established between an identity provider and the services that rely on it, via protocols such as SAML, OAuth, and OpenID Connect.

Hardening — configuring a system to be defensible by removing unnecessary services, closing ports, and applying secure settings.

High availability — deploying firewalls or other critical devices in synchronized pairs or clusters so that one can take over if another fails.

IDS / IPS — intrusion detection (alerts on attacks) and intrusion prevention (actively blocks them) systems, using signature and anomaly methods.

Kill chain — a model of an attack as a sequence of stages, from reconnaissance to actions on objectives, that defenders can break at any single point.

Least privilege — granting each user, process, and account only the access it needs, to contain the damage of any compromise.

Microsegmentation — segmentation taken to a fine grain, often per workload, to minimize the blast radius of a compromise and obstruct lateral movement.

MFA — multi-factor authentication; requiring two or more factors of different types, the single highest-value common control.

NAT / PAT — network address translation and its port-based form, which rewrite addresses and ports as traffic crosses a firewall, conserving public addresses and abstracting internal addressing.

PAM — privileged access management; the extra-careful handling of administrative and other high-power accounts through vaulting, just-in-time access, and session recording.

Penetration testing / red teaming — active testing by skilled humans of whether systems can be compromised, and whether defenders detect and respond.

PKI — public key infrastructure; the certificate authorities and certificates that bind identities to public keys and enable trust at scale.

Post-quantum cryptography — new algorithms designed to resist attack by quantum computers.

Prompt injection — smuggling instructions into content an AI system processes, causing it to ignore its intended constraints.

Risk — the potential for harm, understood as how likely a threat is to exploit a vulnerability combined with how much the result would hurt.

SASE / SSE — secure access service edge, the cloud-delivered convergence of networking and security at the edge near users, and its security-only subset.

SD-WAN — software-defined wide-area networking, which controls and steers wide-area traffic in software over a mix of links, the networking foundation of SASE.

Security policy (firewall) — the ordered set of rules defining what traffic is permitted between zones and what inspection is applied, evaluated top to bottom.

Security profiles — the bundles of deeper inspection a firewall applies to allowed traffic, scanning for malware, exploits, disallowed files, data loss, and URL category.

Security zone — a named grouping of firewall interfaces and networks, the unit in which firewall policy is expressed.

SIEM — security information and event management; centralizes and correlates logs to detect attacks.

SOAR — security orchestration, automation, and response; runs automated playbooks to respond at machine speed and free analysts for judgment.

User identification — a next-generation firewall's ability to tie traffic to the actual user behind it rather than to a shifting IP address, enabling durable, auditable policy.

VPN — virtual private network; an encrypted tunnel protecting data crossing untrusted networks.

Vulnerability management — the ongoing cycle of finding, prioritizing by contextual risk, fixing, and verifying the fixing of weaknesses.

Zero trust — the principle that no user or device is trusted by network location alone, and that every access is verified explicitly under least privilege with breach assumed.